with Richmond Learning Platform

RICHMOND PRACTICE TESTS
for
IELTS

STUDENT'S BOOK with answers

Language Testing

COLLECTION 1

 **Richmond**

Contents

Introduction

This book will prepare you for the International English Language Testing System (IELTS).

It contains four complete paper-based practice tests for the Academic module (Listening, Speaking, Academic Reading and Academic Writing) and two Reading and Writing components for the General Training module (which uses the same Listening and Speaking components as the Academic module). These tests, plus two further Academic tests, are also available online.

The tests in this book and online should be used for practice purposes in the weeks before you take IELTS. The tests will help you practise the kinds of tasks you will be required to complete in the test, within the time limit for each component. When you finish the last practice test, you should feel confident about your ability to work quickly and accurately.

For online practice, go to the **Richmond Learning Platform** to access interactive versions of the tests in this book plus two extra Academic tests. The online tests also provide a step-by-step guide to IELTS, helpful information about each component and tips to help with exam technique. The audio material for all the tests in this book is also available as downloadable audio files.

How to access the Richmond Learning Platform

Go to www.richmondelt.com/practiceIELTS, follow the registration instructions and enter the access code at the front of this book.

Test structure

You can choose between IELTS Academic and IELTS General Training. The difference between the two is in the topics and tasks in the Reading and Writing components. The Listening and Speaking components are the same in both Academic and General Training.

Each test in this book contains the four components which comprise the Academic module: Listening, Academic Reading, Academic Writing and Speaking. You are advised to do the papers in the order in which you will take them in the test itself. However, the Speaking component does not have to be completed on the same day as the other components.

Paper	Time	Content
Listening	30 minutes	Four recorded monologues and conversations with tasks
Academic Reading	60 minutes	Three long reading passages with tasks
Academic Writing	60 minutes	Two writing tasks
Speaking	11–14 minutes	Face-to-face interview

Results

There is no pass or fail in IELTS. Results are reported on a 9-band scale from 0 *(Did not attempt the test)* to 9 *(Expert user)*. You will receive a band score for each component (Listening, Reading, Writing and Speaking), and an overall band score which is the average of the four individual scores.

For further information:
http://www.ielts.org/

Test 1

SECTION 1   Questions 1–10

Complete the notes below.

Write **ONE WORD AND/OR A NUMBER** *for each answer.*

PHOTOGRAPHY COURSE

COURSE DETAILS:

Example	Answer
The course is for	*beginners*

Classes are on **1** .... evenings from 8 p.m. to 10 p.m.

First day of course is on **2** .... September

Cost of the course – **3** £ ....

Studios are on **4** .... Road

TOPICS COVERED ON THE COURSE:

- introduction to **5** .... photography
- photographing people, **6** .... and nature
- developing your own **7** ....

TRIPS:

- photographing life on the **8** .... in the city centre
- photographing birds and animals in the country park

END OF COURSE:

Public visit the exhibition in the school's **9** .... to look at students' work. Visitors vote for their favourite picture.

Winner gets **10** .... on a different course or designer photo frames.

SECTION 2   Questions 11–20

Questions 11–16

*Choose the correct letter, **A**, **B** or **C**.*

11 What is the first thing the new employees will do on the training day?

A learn about their different jobs

B go on a tour of the hotel

C have some refreshments

12 Vanessa says that guests return to Torby Hotel because

A the staff are very friendly.

B they feel as if they are at home.

C they receive special attention.

13 Which form will the new employees give to Vanessa at the training day?

A the contract of employment

B the medical questionnaire

C the bank details form

14 How will the new employees learn about health and safety procedures?

A by watching a film

B by reading the employees' guide

C by listening to a talk

15 What is the purpose of the team-building exercises the new employees will do?

A to find out about their colleagues

B to improve their management skills

C to learn how to deal with customer complaints

16 What will happen on the employees' first day at work?

A They will be introduced to their manager.

B They will learn certain job skills.

C They will collect their uniform.

Questions 17 and 18

*Choose **TWO** letters, **A–E**.*

According to Vanessa, which **TWO** things make the hotel's employees good at customer service?

    A   predicting what customers want

    B   learning quickly from their mistakes

    C   being totally reliable

    D   listening carefully to requests

    E   accepting new ideas

Questions 19 and 20

*Choose **TWO** letters, **A–E**.*

Which **TWO** benefits can employees enjoy?

    A   free transport to and from work

    B   paid holidays

    C   free accommodation

    D   discounted restaurant meals

    E   free use of hotel gym and pool

SECTION 3   *Questions 21–30*

Questions 21 and 22

*Choose **TWO** letters, **A–E**.*

Why do Justin and Myra decide not to design a musical instrument?

    A   They lack musical knowledge.

    B   They prefer computer-based music.

    C   It would be hard to think of an idea.

    D   Musical instruments are expensive.

    E   The market would be too small.

Questions 23 and 24

*Choose **TWO** letters, **A–E**.*

Why do Justin and Myra agree to design a toy?

    A   New toys are always popular.

    B   A lot of money is spent on toys.

    C   Toys come in a range of prices.

    D   There are toys in their homes.

    E   Designing a toy would be fun.

Questions 25–30

Complete the table.

*Write **NO MORE THAN TWO WORDS AND/OR A NUMBER**.*

PROJECT PLAN	Justin	Myra
Market Research	Go to brother's **25** .... and talk to parents.	Design questionnaire for sister's **26** ....
Design	Collect a range of **27** .... from local sources.	Produce a model made of **28** ....
Advertising	Start writing a **29** .... for a commercial.	Design a poster which is **30** ....

Complete the notes below.

*Write **ONE WORD ONLY** for each answer.*

What is personality?

Definition: our pattern of thoughts, feelings and behaviours

Basic characteristics of personality:

- it is constant, e.g. we always react angrily to our noisy **31** ....
- it influences actions, e.g. we give way to **32** .... at a repeated annoyance
- it is shaped by psychological and biological factors
- it is expressed through behaviours, emotions and thoughts: these affect our

  33 .... and how we act in public

Behaviour:

Definition: how we react to our social and physical environment

- Our facial expression, **34** .... , and speech express emotion
- Psychologists believe behaviour is affected by internal or external factors

Public and private behaviour:

- We can't control perceptions of us based on age, race or **35** ....
- Other people's **36** .... about us affect the way we treat people and how they react

Physical attributes:

- Our speech, walk and eye contact affect what people think: e.g. a person who speaks loudly

  may be described as **37** ' .... '

Other characteristics:

- Attitude, e.g. being friendly or standoffish
- Response, e.g. being **38** .... or thoughtful
- General mindset, e.g. being upbeat or moody
- Acting differently with different people, e.g. a **39** .... or good friend

Our private selves:

- Our dreams, **40** .... and moral code
- Our ideas, internal monologue and thoughts
- We decide whether to share these or not

ACADEMIC READING

READING PASSAGE 1

*You should spend about 20 minutes on **Questions 1–13**, which are based on Reading Passage 1 below.*

Where shall we go and eat?

We take restaurants so much for granted these days that it's hard to imagine a world without them. Yet of course that was the case many years ago. When our hunter-gatherer ancestors went out to kill their evening meal, to take home for cooking over the fire, they weren't able to go into the nearest restaurant, where the killing and cooking had already been done for them.

One common type of food outlet nowadays is the takeaway, where the customer chooses dishes from a range of options – a menu – and takes them away to eat. Another is a café or restaurant where each group of guests sit at a table, usually one that they have to themselves, choose from the menu and eat on the premises. But how did such facilities come about?

Possibly the earliest fast-food restaurants were the *thermopolia* in ancient Roman towns. In the town of Pompeii – destroyed by an eruption of Mount Vesuvius in AD 79 – over 150 of these buildings have been identified. They were small shops opening onto the street, with a counter at the front that had large storage vessels built into it. Hot and cold food and drinks were sold, such as hot

sausages, bread, cheese, nuts, dates and wine. The *thermopolia* were in busy public areas, and residents of the town bought a takeaway during their working day or in the evening, particularly if, as was common, they had no cooking facilities of their own.

Some *thermopolia* also had back rooms where customers could sit down to eat. In some cases rooms were hired for private dinners, perhaps when the host's own home was too small for guests. In many cultures nowadays, it is still common to take friends to a restaurant for dinner, rather than cook for them at home. In Pompeii, archaeologists investigating one particular *thermopolium* discovered over a thousand coins – thought to be the day's takings.

Establishments for eating are known to have existed in China from the eleventh century, in the cities of Kaifeng and Hangzhou. These were sizeable towns – Hangzhou may have had a population of over a million, and is thought to have been the largest city in the world in 1180. It had tea houses and taverns that mostly provided refreshments for travellers from other parts of the country, and restaurants with waiter service catering for both travellers and local people. The latter were mainly patronised by the wealthy. They varied in terms of the type of food they offered and the price range. Some had menus, at least for a first course.

In England, taverns serving food were established as early as the eighth century, and cookshops were common in London and other cities by the twelfth century. One London cookshop was praised by a contemporary because not only was it convenient for visitors to the city, but also for local people with unexpected visitors: they could use the cookshop as a takeaway. In the sixteenth century, inns and taverns started to offer a meal each day at a fixed time and price, usually with a special dish. Guests would all sit at the same table and help themselves to whatever was served – there was no question of ordering food. This meal was called the ordinary, and in time both inn dining rooms and other eating places came to be called ordinaries. For the poor without their own cooking facilities, cookshops offered stale bread, cheese and sometimes meat, while street vendors sold cheap snacks.

Luxury eating houses began to develop in the seventeenth century as London's population grew dramatically, providing plenty of customers for the numerous eateries. At many, particularly inns and taverns, customers could take their own ingredients and have them cooked. However, the restaurant in a more recognisably modern form dates from the eighteenth century, and developed in France. Before the upheaval of the French Revolution that began in 1789, restaurants sold food to people who were not well: the meat-based food was intended to 'restore' the person's strength. The French word for 'to restore' is 'restaurer', giving rise to the word 'restaurant'.

One of the earliest French restaurants was founded by Antoine Beauvilliers in Paris in 1782. He served food at small individual tables during specified periods, and listed the dishes available on a menu. His restaurant was described as combining the four essential elements of dining: an elegant room, smart waiters, a good wine selection and excellent cooking.

After the French Revolution, the modern restaurant industry developed rapidly, catering for both local people and travellers. One reason was the relaxation of pre-Revolutionary laws granting monopolies to certain trades, such as pastry makers and butchers. Another was the emergence of middle-class customers with an inclination to dine out. Thirdly, with the destruction of the aristocracy during the Revolution, many of the chefs and cooks they had employed lost their jobs, and some set up restaurants.

Other reasons for this development included the popularity of English fashions, one of which was eating in taverns; and the large number of deputies to parliament coming from the provinces and not having a home of their own in Paris. By 1804 there were 500 restaurants in the city, and before long, restaurants had become commonplace in many countries.

Questions 1–4

Complete the notes below.

Choose **ONE WORD ONLY** from the text for each answer.

Write your answers in boxes 1–4 on your answer sheet.

Thermopolia in Pompeii
- Shopfront had a **1** .... , where food was served from containers
- Situated in public areas, and mostly had **2** .... as customers
- Many **3** .... have been found in one thermopolium

China
- Tea houses and taverns were mostly used by **4** ....

Questions 5–7

Answer the questions below.

Choose **NO MORE THAN TWO WORDS** from the text for each answer.

Write your answers in boxes 5–7 on your answer sheet.

London

5 What name was given to a meal that customers of an inn or tavern shared?

6 What could be bought in the street?

7 What was increasing in seventeenth-century London that benefited eating houses?

Questions 8–13

Do the following statements agree with the information given in Reading Passage 1?

In boxes 8–13 on your answer sheet, write

TRUE	if the statement agrees with the information
FALSE	if the statement contradicts the information
NOT GIVEN	if there is no information on this

Restaurants in France

8 Pre-revolutionary restaurants worked in the same way as London eating houses.

9 Meals in Beauvilliers's restaurant were available at fixed times of day.

10 Beauvilliers's restaurant was generally considered the best in Paris.

11 The first monopolies over food were introduced after the Revolution.

12 The chefs in some restaurants had previously worked for aristocrats.

13 Deputies coming to parliament expected to be able to eat food from their home region.

You should spend about 20 minutes on **Questions 14–26**, which are based on Reading Passage 2 below.

Isambard Kingdom
Brunel

Royal Albert Bridge
Clifton Bridge
· Paddington Station

a major figure in the field of engineering

A Isambard Kingdom Brunel (1806–1859) was one of the most inventive and prolific figures in engineering history. He built twenty-five railways lines, over a hundred bridges (including five suspension bridges), eight pier and dock systems, three ships and a pre-fabricated army field hospital.

B Brunel was born into his profession. His father, Marc (1769–1849), was one of the great engineers of the Industrial Revolution and a pioneer of mechanical production. Born in France, Marc moved to England in 1799, married and had a son, Isambard, who was born in 1806. Marc made sure that the boy had a theoretical education as well as a practical engineering apprenticeship. Isambard attended school in England, but as the best mathematical education at that time was to be found in France, he was sent to college there in 1820.

C Marc invented many mechanical devices, including knitting machines and marine steam engines, as well as designing the Thames Tunnel in London: this was the world's first pedestrian tunnel under a river, although since 1869 it has been used by trains. Past attempts had failed, but Marc developed the technique of constructing it under a tunnelling shield. Work started in 1825, and Isambard, who had returned to London in 1822, became resident engineer in 1826. Work was suspended in 1828 when the tunnel was seriously damaged by flooding and Isambard was nearly killed. He was sent to convalesce in Bristol, where he was encouraged to enter a competition to design the Clifton Bridge across the River Avon. He was declared the winner, and he set to work on the bridge.

D In 1833, Isambard Brunel was appointed chief engineer to the Great Western Railway (GWR), and the design of this proposed railway linking Bristol and London absorbed much of his time. Brunel presented an audacious proposal for a high speed railway, on which locomotives could travel at 60 mph (96 km/hr) rather than the usual 35 mph (56 km/hr). He argued that if he developed a track with a gauge (that is, the distance between the rails) of 7 feet 0¼ inches (2,140 mm) – broader than the standard 4 feet 8½ inches (1,435 mm) –

the centre of gravity of the carriages would be lower. This would allow the engines' driving wheels to be larger and the trains to run faster. Brunel's scheme was highly controversial and he fought a bitter battle to implement it: even threatening to resign when the railway's directors tried to force him to work with a co-engineer. The broad gauge was eventually used on the Great Western Railway (GWR), Cornwall Railway and smaller lines, even though an 1845 Royal Commission deemed it too expensive to be adopted as the national standard gauge.

E   Brunel was equally ambitious in the design of the GWR's London terminus, Paddington Station, which he was charged with rebuilding in 1849 to accommodate the crowds expected to converge on London for the 1851 Great Exhibition. He was asked to construct a flexible covered space to accommodate the railway's future needs and to outshine Euston Station, the London terminus of the GWR's arch-rival, the Great Northern Railway, which ran trains between the capital and the north of England. Brunel was inspired by Joseph Paxton's design for the Crystal Palace, which was built to house the Great Exhibition. This consisted of an iron framework covered almost entirely with glass. Brunel hired the same contractors to build a similar three-span structure for Paddington, using the same materials.

F   In an age when the new railways were regarded as the peak of modernity and the source of future prosperity for provincial cities and towns, public interest in Brunel's daring schemes for the GWR was intense. It is difficult for us to comprehend the scale and complexity of the construction of a new railway like the Great Western or Cornish Railway today. One of Brunel's gifts was his ability to understand that, if passengers were to fully appreciate the romance of the railway, its engineering had to be invisible. The trains should float over the landscape with such apparent ease that the passengers did not notice if they were climbing hills or crossing water. To achieve this, Brunel and his team designed numerous viaducts, tunnels, embankments and sea defences.

G   Arguably his greatest challenge – and achievement – was on the Cornish Railway. Here Brunel designed the Royal Albert railway bridge to cross the River Tamar at its narrowest point, allowing sufficient height for sailing vessels to pass underneath. Brunel's solution was a single rail track crossing a two-span suspension bridge supported by piers close to each shore and one central pier.

H   The project faced two particular challenges. The first was to build the pier in the middle of the river, and Brunel solved this by designing a 'great cylinder' to be floated into position, a watertight structure that made it possible to work under water. The second difficulty was to raise the main spans, the two horizontal sections of the bridge. These were built beside the river and floated into position, then raised three feet (90 cm) at a time, allowing the piers supporting them to be built up beneath them. The bridge was completed in 1859, the year of Brunel's death.

Questions 14–18

Reading Passage 2 has eight paragraphs, **A–H**.

Which paragraph contains the following information?

Write the correct letter, **A–H**, in boxes 14–18 on your answer sheet.

NB You may use any letter more than once.

14 a reference to opposition to one of Isambard Kingdom Brunel's proposals

15 how Isambard Kingdom Brunel dealt with problems in the construction of a bridge

16 an outline of Isambard Kingdom Brunel's concept of the ideal experience of travelling by train

17 how Isambard Kingdom Brunel gained a knowledge of engineering

18 how trains could be made to travel more quickly

Questions 19–22

Look at the following statements (Questions 19–22) and the list of structures below.

Match each statement with the correct structure **A–D**.

NB You may use any letter more than once.

Write the correct letter, **A–D**, in boxes 19–22 on your answer sheet.

19 It was modelled on another structure.

20 It used a method of construction invented by Marc Brunel.

21 Its design had to take into account the needs of shipping.

22 Isambard Kingdom Brunel was injured while working on it.

List of Structures

A Thames Tunnel **B** Clifton Bridge **C** Paddington Station **D** Royal Albert Bridge

---

Questions 23–26

Complete the summary below.

Choose **NO MORE THAN TWO WORDS** from the text for each answer.

Write your answers in boxes 23–26 on your answer sheet.

Paddington Station, London

Brunel was responsible for rebuilding London's Paddington Station and making it ready for the large number of people predicted to visit the **23** .... two years later. GWR wanted the station to be **24** .... enough to cope with the requirements that lay ahead and more impressive than the Great Northern Railway's **25** .... in the capital, Euston Station. Brunel's design used **26** .... and .... as the main materials.

READING PASSAGE 3

You should spend about 20 minutes on **Questions 27–40**, which are based on Reading Passage 3 below.

Background music
and
consumer behaviour

Can background music in retail stores, restaurants or nightclubs

exert any influence on consumer choice or behaviour?

While consumers would consider themselves far beyond the influence of such factors, marketing and environmental psychology studies have shown that music has a direct influence on many behaviours below conscious awareness. Psychological research has shown that consumer behaviour is highly sensitive to subtle atmospheric changes in the environment.

A number of studies have illustrated how background music influences consumer behaviour in retail environments. For instance, as long ago as 1993, researchers Areni and Kim showed that customers selected more expensive merchandise in a wine store when exposed to classical music as opposed to pop music. This has a lot to do with priming (that is, being influenced by earlier associations) and how the consumer mind interprets information. We associate classical music with sophistication and affluence; hence shoppers are primed to feel in a more high-class frame of mind. Since music has the ability to prime certain thoughts, which in turn adjust our attitudes, beliefs and behaviours, the presence

of music that primed thoughts of prosperity increased the likelihood of customers buying more expensive wine.

Yacht and Spangenberg (1990) showed that department store customers under 25 perceived their shopping duration as much shorter than it actually was in the presence of pop music (which they were likely to prefer), whereas those over 25 gave a much shorter time estimation of their shopping experience when listening to easy listening music (the probable preference of this age group).

Recent research suggests that the music played in nightclubs may influence the consumption of drinks and other nightclub behaviour. Yale Fox (2010) suggests that while popular songs may attract people to hit the dance floor, it is the slower songs that lead nightclubbers to drink more. Such knowledge is useful to club owners and DJs, as drink sales can be maximised using this formula, given that dancing will cause dehydration and slow songs lead to drink consumption.

Psychological research has indicated that slower tempo, lower volume and familiar music lead to consumers staying slightly longer in stores than those exposed to fast tempo, higher volume and less familiar music (Garlin and Own, 2006). However, other studies have indicated that, although supermarket shoppers tend to shop more slowly in the presence of slower tempo music as opposed to more upbeat music, they do not necessarily buy more items because of it. In fact, shoppers exposed to higher tempo music bought similar amounts of items, but in a shorter space of time. So while sales per minute increased, overall spend was not statistically different.

Restaurant patrons also spend longer in restaurants whilst listening to slow tempo and low volume music. However, this may be an undesirable consumer behaviour: during peak times, restaurant owners do not wish their customers to stay longer than they need to, because it is not profitable. During off-peak hours, though, a slower tempo, low-volume music selection may lead to customers staying longer, which has the added benefit of making the restaurant appear busier.

BAA, an airport operator, once experimented with their soundscape to test the influence of sound on consumer behaviour within a Glasgow airport terminal. Over an eight-week period, they alternated between complete silence and playing a soundtrack of generative music (music generated electronically), birdsong and waves crashing. They found that the soundtrack was associated with a 10% increase in sales for the airport shops.

Classic economic theory stresses that consumers make decisions in a logical and rational way, undertaking a cost-benefit analysis. This would suggest that consumer behaviour is exempt from the influence of such atmospheric cues as background music. However, environmental psychology studies point out that very slight changes in the retail environment can dramatically shape consumer behaviour and consumer psychology. This is more evidence to support the behavioural economics viewpoint that, in fact, much of what consumers do is rather irrational, and is largely driven by how they unconsciously process the external environment.

Although consumers do not walk around a store evaluating the music at a conscious level, background music is able to affect emotions beyond recognition and exert a powerful unconscious influence over consumer behaviour. While consumers may be aware of their change in mood, they are unlikely to attribute the feelings directly to the music itself.

Despite background music being highly controllable and an easy factor to adjust for any company, many service providers fail to optimise this in-store marketing technique, for a number of reasons. Firstly, atmospheric cues are often chosen by managers to suit their own preferences rather than on the basis of scientific experimentation. Secondly, the way in which most companies would test the influence of their retail environment on consumer behaviour is likely to be through attitudinal surveys and other traditional marketing techniques. Acquiring consumer insight in this way largely ignores the unconscious processes that drive their behaviour.

Questions 27–31

*Choose the correct letter, **A**, **B**, **C** or **D**.*

*Write the correct letter, **A–D**, in boxes 27–31 on your answer sheet.*

27 According to the first paragraph, consumers

  A are unhappy about retailers using music to affect their mood.

  B tend to behave in unpredictable ways in psychology studies.

  C do not realise that they are affected by music in retail situations.

  D may choose to go to shops because they like the music being played.

28 The consumers studied by Areni and Kim

  A preferred to hear classical rather than pop music.

  B spent more if they heard music that they connected with wealth.

  C preferred to hear music that they associated with their childhood.

  D spent longer in the store if they enjoyed the music being played.

29 What did Yacht and Spangenberg conclude?

  A People under 25 tended to remain in stores for longer than those over 25.

  B Many stores missed opportunities to use music as a way of attracting customers.

  C Customers under 25 spent more money in stores than those over 25.

  D The music played in stores affected people's perception of time.

30 What do Yale Fox's findings show?

  A how nightclub owners can influence the sale of drinks

  B why some types of music are more popular than others in nightclubs

  C why slow music reduces the sale of drinks in nightclubs

  D how to attract more people to nightclubs

31 What point is made in the fifth paragraph about shoppers in supermarkets?

  A Music may make them feel more critical of their surroundings.

  B Fast music generally increases the quantity of goods that they buy.

  C Music has a more stressful effect on them than was previously thought.

  D The tempo of music does not seem to affect the amount they spend.

Questions 32–36

Do the following statements agree with the claims of the writer in Reading Passage 3?

In boxes 32–36 on your answer sheet, write

YES	*if the statement agrees with the claims of the writer*
NO	*if the statement contradicts the claims of the writer*
NOT GIVEN	*if it is impossible to say what the writer thinks about this*

32 Slow music played in a restaurant has advantages and disadvantages at different times.

33 BAA expected consumer spending to rise when they played a soundtrack.

34 BAA's experiment led them to make permanent changes in their soundscape.

35 Behavioural economics emphasises the illogical factors in consumer behaviour.

36 Consumers can usually identify background music as the cause of changes in their mood.

Questions 37–40

*Complete each sentence with the correct ending **A**–**E** below.*

*Write the correct letter, **A**–**E**, in boxes 37–40 on your answer sheet.*

37 According to classic economic theory, consumers base their decisions on

38 According to behavioural economics, consumers are affected by

39 Managers of retail outlets are likely to choose background music on the basis of

40 Research in the form of surveys may miss

A	personal taste.
B	an assessment of advantages and drawbacks.
C	significant influences on consumer behaviour.
D	changes in their preferences.
E	subtle differences in their surroundings.

ACADEMIC WRITING

WRITING TASK 1

You should spend about 20 minutes on this task.

> The graph and chart below show the average monthly maximum temperatures and the average monthly rainfall in two Australian cities, Darwin and Sydney.
>
> Summarise the information by selecting and reporting the main features, and make comparisons where relevant.

Write at least 150 words.

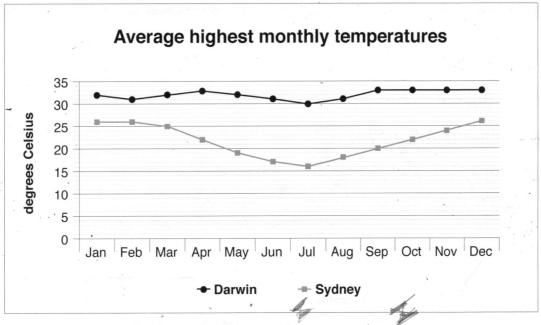

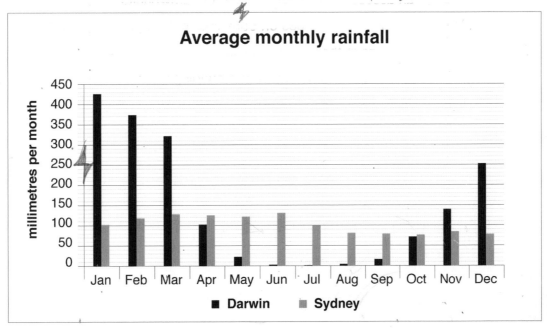

WRITING TASK 2

You should spend about 40 minutes on this task.

Write about the following topic:

> **Many people seem to lead very busy lives, and have much less free time than they would like.**
>
> **What do you think are the causes of this situation? What measures could be taken to improve it?**

Give reasons for your answer and include any relevant examples from your own knowledge or experience.

Write at least 250 words.

SPEAKING

PART 1   INTRODUCTION AND INTERVIEW

The examiner will introduce himself/herself and check your identification. Here is an example:

Can you tell me your full name, please?
And what shall I call you?

The examiner will then ask some questions on familiar topics such as where you live, your work or studies, your family and your interests. Here are some examples:

Your home country

• Let's talk about your home country. Which country do you live in now?
• Which area in your country do you like most? [Why?]

PART 2   INDIVIDUAL LONG TURN

The examiner will give you a topic on a card and you have to talk about the topic for one or two minutes. You have one minute to think about what you want to say. You can make some notes to help you if you wish.

Here is an example of a candidate task card:

> **Helping people**
> Describe a time when a person helped you.
> You should say:
>   who the person was
>   how you knew this person
>   when this person helped you
> and how this person helped you.

PART 3   DISCUSSION

The examiner will ask you some general questions which relate to the topic in Part 2. Here are some examples:

Helping people

What help can people who live together give each other every day?
What are the advantages of asking for help from family members rather than friends?
Whose responsibility is it to care for the rising number of old people in most societies?

Test 2

SECTION 1   *Questions 1–10*

Complete the form below.

*Write **NO MORE THAN TWO WORDS AND/OR A NUMBER** for each answer.*

Police Form – Theft

Example	*Answer*
First Name:	<u>Sabrina</u>

Surname:	**1** ....
Contact phone number:	07188 233764

Description of stolen item

Stolen item:	**2** ....
Value:	**3** £ ....
Colour:	**4** ....

Details of theft

Date:	**5** ....
Time:	8:30 a.m.
Place:	**6** ....
Witnesses:	her **7** ....
Description of thief:	tall with **8** ....
Other experiences of theft in same area:	friend lost his **9** ....

Insurance

Type of policy:	**10** ' .... '

SECTION 2   Questions 11–20

Questions 11–15

Complete the notes below.

Write **NO MORE THAN TWO WORDS AND/OR A NUMBER** for each answer.

> ■ ■ ■ ■ ■ ■ **Facts about Fairlight College** ■ ■ ■ ■ ■ ■
>
> ■ has 2,500 students and **11** .... teachers.
> ■ buildings initially used as a **12** ....
> ■ college Mission Statement: **13** ' ....'
> ■ college has connections with **14** ....
> ■ Freshers' Ball on 5th Oct at the **15** .... Club.

Questions 16–20

Label the plan below.

Write the correct letter, **A–I**, next to questions 16–20.

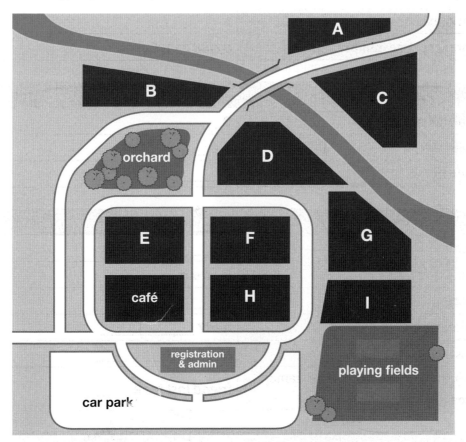

16	Sports Centre	....	
17	Library	....	
18	Innovation Centre	....	
19	Science Block	....	
20	Canteen	....	

SECTION 3   Questions 21–30

Questions 21–25

Choose the correct letter, A, B or C.

21 How long can Metin talk to the tutor for?

    A 10 minutes

    B 20 minutes

    C half an hour

22 Why did Metin decide to focus on bridge construction?

    A Anyone can build a bridge.

    B Bridges have a long history.

    C He admires some modern bridges.

23 Metin and his tutor agree that his 'bridges around the world' idea is too

    A theoretical.

    B unoriginal.

    C broad.

24 To get a good mark for the assignment, Metin should

    A provide a clear overview.

    B write enough words.

    C examine one aspect in depth.

25 What does Metin's tutor suggest he does at home?

    A look again at his sources

    B talk to other students

    C write down some key ideas

Questions 26–29

What do the speakers say about each of these bridges?

*Match the types of bridge **26–29** with the comments **A–F**.*

Comments
A They were designed long before the first one was built.
B Extra support is needed during construction.
C They cannot extend as far as some other bridges.
D They have been made using natural materials.
E The design is unsuitable for certain locations.
F They may be called by a different name.

Types of Bridge

26   suspension bridges   ....

27   arch bridges   ....

28   beam bridges   ....

29   cable-stayed bridges   ....

Question 30

*Choose the correct letter, **A**, **B** or **C**.*

30   Metin asks if he can

    A   see his tutor next week.

    B   write a first draft for his tutor.

    C   send a new plan to his tutor.

SECTION 4   Questions 31–40

Complete the sentences below.

Write **NO MORE THAN TWO WORDS AND/OR A NUMBER** *for each answer.*

Starlings

- Starlings are medium-sized birds.
- Their **31** .... have a metallic appearance.

Starling murmurations

- A murmuration can look like a large **32** ....
- The time of year that murmurations are largest is in **33** ....
- Every day, groups of starlings go out to look for **34** ....
- In 2008, scientists studied starlings using **35** .... that were linked together.
- Starlings can fly very fast, so it's important they don't have a **36** ....
- A small change in the flight of one bird is **37** .... throughout the group.

Starling populations

- In the UK, starling numbers are so low that they have gone onto the **38** ....
- Starlings are barely mentioned in eighteenth-century **39** ....
- In 1890, an American introduced starlings to **40** .... in New York.

ACADEMIC READING

READING PASSAGE 1

*You should spend about 20 minutes on **Questions 1–13**, which are based on Reading Passage 1 below.*

Traditional domestic gardens of China

In China, gardens of various types have a long history, dating back more than three thousand years to the large parks of the emperors and aristocracy. Smaller domestic gardens were first constructed in the fifth or sixth century AD. They are often called 'literati gardens', because many were created for the country's elite – the scholar-gentlemen, or literati, who worked as officials in the administration of the empire. The number of gardens increased steadily from the twelfth century, particularly in southern China, thanks to the temperate climate and wealth of the region, reaching a peak in the sixteenth century.

Garden design was traditionally seen as a serious art form comparable with painting, sculpture and poetry. Designers aimed to create a landscape in miniature, providing the sensation of wandering through the natural world: arrangements of rocks evoked mountain ranges, trees suggested forests, and ponds represented seas. Gardens were intended to reflect balance and harmony between human beings and nature.

European gardens of the eighteenth and nineteenth centuries were characterised by flowerbeds, lawns and wide, panoramic views. Chinese gardens, on the other hand, contained viewing points presenting numerous small vistas, perfectly composed and framed – as though the visitor is looking at a painting. The idea was that different scenes would be revealed to visitors as they walked round – a pond, tree or waterfall, perhaps, viewed through the window of a pavilion or gallery. Buildings were an integral part of the Chinese garden, again unlike gardens in Europe.

According to Ji Cheng, who wrote on garden design in the early seventeenth century, gardens should 'look natural, though man-made'. He also emphasised the harmonious combination of opposites, such as small and large, revelation and concealment. For this reason, irregularly shaped rocks were often placed next to smooth, rectangular clay tiles, or a dark entrance led into a sun-lit courtyard. In Chinese gardens, beautiful compositions were created, whereas in European gardens of that period there was an emphasis on symmetry and formality, with straight rows of trees that often seemed as unlike nature as possible.

The classic domestic garden in China was a rectangular outdoor space adjoining a home. It was enclosed by walls or buildings and had no windows on the outside walls. Being enclosed provided privacy and a degree of protection from the summer sun and winter cold. Walls were often painted white, to set off the flowers and trees. There might be a pond in the centre of the garden, with buildings beside it. Gardens varied in size, from less than a hectare to more than ten. Some were large enough to contain orchards or fields to grow produce which could be sold.

As well as plants, rocks and water, gardens traditionally contained pavilions, temples, towers and other buildings. These were often linked by covered galleries that zigzagged or wound round the edge of the pond, and provided shelter from the sun and rain. The galleries usually contained small windows, framing carefully planned views of the garden. The windows might be circular, oval, or in the shape of a leaf or petal. Like the galleries, bridges, too, were rarely straight. Footpaths often contained designs made with coloured pebbles, such as a crane – a bird symbolising good luck – or a fishing net denoting wealth. There were also scenes from well-known legends.

Gardens were intended to be elegant and beautiful, and to reflect the wealth and status of the homeowner. Designing gardens became an activity of the wealthy and well-

educated, whatever their knowledge. Like gardens elsewhere in the world, they were used for relaxation and entertaining guests, but there has always been a much greater emphasis than in Europe on the garden as a calm setting for solitude and contemplation, and for activities such as painting, poetry, calligraphy, music and study. Some scholar-gentlemen in effect withdrew from the outside world and retreated to their gardens.

One of the most impressive Chinese gardens, and a UNESCO World Heritage Site since 1997, is the Humble Administrator's Garden in the city of Suzhou, close to Shanghai. This was constructed between 1510 and 1526 by Wang Xiancheng, an imperial envoy, on his retirement, and it takes its name from a line in a poem written some three hundred years earlier. The garden is dominated by a pond – large and irregularly shaped – and 48 structures for viewing different scenes or for entertainment. These include a waterside pavilion built partly on land and partly on stilts over the pond. After Wang's death, the garden changed hands many times and was split up, eventually into three separate properties. The whole of the original garden came under the same ownership in 1949 and was later restored.

In recent years, a number of Chinese gardens have been created in other countries, particularly in cities with a large Chinese community, such as Vancouver, Canada and Sydney, Australia. Sydney's Chinese Garden of Friendship was officially opened in 1988 to mark the country's bicentenary.

Questions 1–9

Do the following statements agree with the information given in Reading Passage 1?

In boxes 1–9 on your answer sheet, write

TRUE	if the statement agrees with the information
FALSE	if the statement contradicts the information
NOT GIVEN	if there is no information on this

1   The earliest domestic gardens in China are thought to have been created three thousand years ago.

2   Many Chinese domestic gardens belonged to government officials.

3   Gardens were often represented in Chinese paintings.

4   Panoramic views were typical of both European and Chinese gardens.

5   The design of Chinese domestic gardens was influenced by the weather.

6   In Chinese gardens, galleries normally connected buildings by the shortest route.

7   Designs in footpaths were sometimes based on paintings.

8   Garden design was limited to professional designers.

9   Gardens were sometimes used for the performance of plays.

Questions 10–13

Choose **NO MORE THAN TWO WORDS** from the text for each answer.

Write your answers in boxes 10–13 on your answer sheet.

10   What is a view in a Chinese garden compared with?

11   What were sometimes situated beside clay tiles?

12   Where does the name of the Humble Administrator's Garden come from?

13   What occupies a large part of the Humble Administrator's Garden?

READING PASSAGE 2

*You should spend about 20 minutes on **Questions 14–26**, which are based on Reading Passage 2 below.*

What a **coincidence**

We're so often surprised when two similar things happen at the same time for no obvious reason. But is that surprise always justified?

A   Many families write an annual round-robin – one letter, with identical copies sent to numerous 'friends'. This consists of annoying tales of their brilliant children and winter holidays in the sun, of interest only to themselves, and which is only matched by the dullness of hearing about the coincidences they have experienced such as bumping into their next-door neighbour in Antarctica. These may seem to be amazing events to the people concerned – though not to anybody else – but in fact they may be far less unusual than we think.

B   Unlikely things happen extremely frequently. Last Saturday, I bought a lottery ticket using the random lucky-dip process and got the numbers 2, 12, 15, 25, 32 and 47, and when the lottery was drawn, one of the six numbers was 15. Amazing? No, you say. The probability of twelve particular numbers coming up is one in 200 trillion – the same chance as flipping a coin 48 times and it coming up heads every time. Yet because the two sets of figures are mostly different, we aren't impressed by the low probability of their occurrence.

C   Even rather remarkable events can be unsurprising. Take the 2010 story in the British media about the Allali family, whose third child Sami was born on the same date – 7 October – as her older brother Adam (aged three) and sister Najla (aged five). The *Daily Mail* newspaper said this was a 1 in 48,000,000 event – a number obtained by multiplying three 1 in 365 events together. This number is misleading for two reasons. First, it is wrong: this would be the chance of all three children being born on a pre-specified date of 7 October (and also makes the rather strong assumption of random birth dates, and hence conceptions, throughout the year). Since the first child, Najla, set the date, she does not feature as part of the coincidence, and so the appropriate calculation is 1/365 x 1/365, which is a 1 in 133,000 chance. This is not terribly exciting, as there are 1,000,000 families with three children under 18 in the UK, and so we would expect around seven other examples to exist at any time. This also means there are about 167,000 third children born each year, and so we would expect the event to be reported roughly annually. This duly happens, and the *Daily Mail* wrote the same story about the MacKriell family in 2008 (but this time getting the odds right).

D   The more deflationary way of measuring 'impressiveness' is to take the chance of a specific event and then multiply it by the number of opportunities for a similar such event to occur. And there is always a vast number of possible coincidences that could happen, but don't. For example, there is a 1 in 14,000,000 chance of any particular ticket winning the lottery, which is tiny, but they sell 30,000,000 tickets each draw, and so we expect on average two people to win each week. The 'birthday paradox' is a classic example, where only 23 people are needed to have more than a 50:50 chance that two share the same birthday, owing to there being 23 x 22/2 = 253 possible 'pairings'.

E   And maybe some coincidences are not as unlikely as claimed. Many top 10 coincidence lists include John Adams (2nd US president) and Thomas Jefferson (3rd US president) both dying on 4 July 1826, the 50th anniversary of the Declaration of Independence. Even if we assume the families honestly reported the dates, some people on their deathbeds have been known to hold on to life until a significant anniversary – James Monroe (5th US president) also died on 4 July.

F   People tell stories to themselves, make connections, claim a mysterious power of synchrony and seem unwilling to admit that things could have been different. A standard coincidence story is about how people met their partner: what if they had not gone on that date, what if the car had not broken down outside the farm with the beautiful daughter? They regard these events as coincidences on the basis of the outcome, yet if the events had played out otherwise, the people concerned would have seen those as equally being 'coincidences'. The fact that something happens and leads to something else doesn't make it a coincidence.

G   There is a strong tendency to believe that things are as they are for a purpose, to find patterns and meaning in our lives. Perhaps the greatest coincidence, both for its unlikeliness and for its importance, is that we are here at all, both as a species or as individuals. Each one of us exists due to a single extraordinary event that might well not have happened. But pondering the possibility of non-existence is quite tricky and, unsurprisingly, we tend to avoid it.

Questions 14–18

Reading Passage 2 has seven paragraphs, **A–G**.

Which paragraph contains the following information?

Write the correct letter, **A–G**, in boxes 14–18 on your answer sheet.

NB You may use any letter more than once.

14 a reference to the probability of a coincidence being miscalculated

15 an example of events being seen as coincidences because of what they led to

16 a mention of two events that are equally unlikely to happen

17 a claim that coincidences only interest the people who are directly involved

18 a mention of similar unlikely events occurring in different families

Questions 19 and 20

Choose **TWO** letters, **A–E**.

Write the correct letters in boxes 19 and 20 on your answer sheet.

Which **TWO** of these events are said to be more common than most people realise?

A   meeting a neighbour in Antarctica

B   buying a lottery ticket with particular numbers

C   three siblings sharing the same birthday

D   people dying on a significant date

E   meeting a partner because a car broke down

Questions 21–26

Complete the sentences below.

Choose **ONE WORD ONLY** from the passage for each answer.

Write your answers in boxes 21–26 on your answer sheet.

21   Round-robins are known for the .... of the news they include.

22   Unlikely events occur more .... than is generally realised.

23   Stories about siblings born on the same date are likely to occur once a ....

24   It is a well-known .... that relatively few people are required for any two of them to share a birthday.

25   On three occasions, an American .... has died on 4 July.

26   People are unlikely to think about ...., because it is difficult to do so.

READING PASSAGE 3

You should spend about 20 minutes on **Questions 27–40**, which are based on Reading Passage 3 below.

Why comparisons of medical treatment are essential

Medical treatment is relevant to virtually everyone at some time in their life, and of course patients and healthcare professionals hope that treatments will be helpful. These optimistic expectations can have a very positive effect on everybody's satisfaction with healthcare, as the British doctor Richard Asher noted in one of his essays for doctors:

'If you can believe fervently in your treatment, even though controlled tests show that it is quite useless, then your results look much better, your patients feel much better, and your income is much better too. I believe this accounts for the remarkable success of some of the less gifted, but more credulous members of our profession, and also for the violent dislike of statistics and controlled tests which fashionable and successful doctors are accustomed to display' (Asher, 1972).

People often recover from illness without any specific treatment: nature and time are great healers. The progress and outcome of illness if left untreated must obviously be taken into account when treatments are being tested: treatment may improve or it may worsen outcomes. Writers over the centuries have drawn attention to the need to be sceptical about claims that treatments can be more effective than nature. Put another way, 'If you leave a dose of 'flu to nature, you'll probably get over it in a week; but if you go to the doctor, you'll recover in a mere seven days.'

In the knowledge that much illness is self-limiting, doctors sometimes prescribe 'dummy' treatments in the hope that their patients will derive psychological benefit – the so-called placebo effect. Patients may be given a placebo and, because they believe that it will help to relieve their symptoms – even though the treatment, in fact, has no physical effects – may well feel better.

Doctors have recognised the importance of using placebos for centuries. For example, William Cullen referred to his use of a placebo as long ago as 1772 (Cullen, 1772), and references to placebos increased during the nineteenth century (e.g. Cummings, 1805; Forbes, 1846). Because Austin Flint believed that orthodox drug treatment was usurping the credit due to 'nature', he gave thirteen patients with rheumatism a 'placeboic remedy' consisting of a highly dilute extract of the bark of the quassia tree. The result was that 'the favourable progress of the cases was such as to secure for the remedy generally the entire confidence of the patients' (Flint, 1863). At the beginning of the twentieth century, William Rivers discussed psychologically-mediated effects of treatments in detail (Rivers, 1908).

Just as the healing power of nature and the placebo effect have been recognised for centuries, so also has the need for comparisons to assess the effects of treatments over and above natural and psychologically-mediated effects. Sometimes treatment comparisons are made in people's minds: they have an impression that they or others are responding differently to a new treatment compared with previous responses to treatments. For example, Ambroise Paré, a French military surgeon, concluded that treatment of battle wounds with boiling oil (as was common practice) was likely to be harmful. He concluded this when the supply of oil ran out and his patients recovered more quickly than usual (Paré, 1575).

Most of the time, impressions like this need to be followed up by formal investigations, perhaps initially by analysis of healthcare records. Such impressions may then lead to carefully conducted comparisons. The danger arises when impressions alone are used as a guide to treatment recommendations and decisions.

Treatment comparisons based on impressions, or relatively restricted analyses, only provide reliable information in the rare circumstances when treatment effects are dramatic (Glasziou et al., 2007). One such example is the use of adrenaline for life-threatening allergic reactions (McLean-Tooke et al., 2003). Most medical treatments don't have such dramatic effects as this, however, and unless care is taken to avoid biased comparisons, dangerously mistaken conclusions about the effects of treatment may result.

Comparing treatments given today with those given in the past only rarely provides a secure basis for a fair test (Behring et al., 1893), because relevant factors other than the treatments themselves change over time. If possible, therefore, comparisons should involve giving different treatments at more or less the same time.

A patient may be given different treatments one after the other – a so-called crossover test (Martini, 1932). An early example was reported in 1786 by Dr Caleb Parry in Bath, England. Rhubarb, a vegetable imported from Turkey at considerable expense, was generally prescribed for certain patients. Parry wanted to find out whether there was any reason to pay for this rhubarb, rather than using rhubarb grown locally in England. So he 'crossed-over' the type of rhubarb given to each individual patient at different times and then compared the symptoms each patient experienced while eating each type of rhubarb (Parry, 1786). (He didn't find any advantage in the expensive rhubarb!)

Treatments are usually tested by comparing groups of people who receive different treatments. A comparison of two treatments will be unfair if relatively well people have received one treatment and relatively ill people have received the other, so the experiences of similar groups of people who receive different treatments over the same period of time must be compared. Al-Razi recognised this more than a thousand years ago when, wishing to reach a conclusion about how to treat patients with early signs of meningitis, he treated one group of patients and intentionally withheld treatment from a comparison group (Al-Razi ninth century).

Comparisons with nature or with other treatments are needed for fair tests of treatments. If these comparisons are to be fair, they must address genuine uncertainties, avoid biases and the effects of chance, and be interpreted carefully.

Questions 27–32

*Choose the correct letter, **A**, **B**, **C** or **D**.*

*Write the correct letter, **A–D**, in boxes 27–32 on your answer sheet.*

27 According to Asher, what is likely to make a treatment effective?

    A   the wealth of the patients

    B   the doctor's knowledge of controlled tests

    C   the patient's understanding of medicine

    D   the doctor's confidence in the treatment

28 What does Asher imply about 'fashionable and successful doctors'?

    A   They choose to ignore facts that show their treatments to be useless.

    B   They do not understand the importance of having statistics.

    C   Their patients prefer to be treated by someone who shows them their results.

    D   They would find it hard to explain controlled tests to patients.

29 What point does the writer make in the third paragraph?

    A   Treatment is generally more beneficial than a natural recovery.

    B   Understanding of how people recover from illness has greatly increased over time.

    C   People may recover equally quickly from illness with and without treatment.

    D   Treatments need to be thoroughly tested before they are used.

30 Austin Flint found that patients

    A   lost confidence in doctors who gave them placebos.

    B   wrongly believed it was the quassia bark that had cured them.

    C   generally insisted on receiving orthodox drug treatment.

    D   failed to recover if they realised they had received placebos.

31 In the sixth paragraph, what does the writer imply about Paré?

    A   His assessments of patients' recovery time were inaccurate.

    B   He was unwilling to recognise the benefits of some traditional treatments.

    C   He only questioned treatment when the oil it required became unavailable.

    D   He faced opposition from other doctors when he objected to treatment with boiling oil.

32 In the seventh paragraph, the writer

    A   stresses the need for opinions to be supported by research.

    B   warns against underestimating the value of impressions.

    C   suggests how to improve the design of healthcare records.

    D   outlines the possible effects of poorly thought out treatment decisions.

Questions 33–36

Do the following statements agree with the claims of the writer in Reading Passage 3?

In boxes 33–36 on your answer sheet, write

YES	*if the statement agrees with the claims of the writer*
NO	*if the statement contradicts the claims of the writer*
NOT GIVEN	*if it is impossible to say what the writer thinks about this*

33 Optimism can benefit both patients and the medical profession.

34 Placebos are more effective on mental illness than physical illness.

35 The effectiveness of adrenaline in treating allergic reactions is unusual for a medical treatment.

36 Al-Razi chose an unfair method of comparing treatments.

Questions 37–40

Complete the summary below.

Choose ONE WORD ONLY from the passage for each answer.

CROSSOVER TEST

In the eighteenth century, an English doctor, Caleb Parry, carried out an experiment in the treatment of patients. He gave each patient first one then another type of **37** .... , to find out if they had different effects on the patients' **38** .... He concluded that the usual treatment, which was more **39** .... because it used vegetables grown in Turkey, offered no **40** ....

ACADEMIC WRITING

WRITING TASK 1

You should spend about 20 minutes on this task.

> *The pie charts below show the percentage of goods transported by five different means within a particular country.*
>
> *Summarise the information by selecting and reporting the main features, and make comparisons where relevant.*

Write at least 150 words.

Modes of transport used to move goods between eastern region and rest of country (percentages)

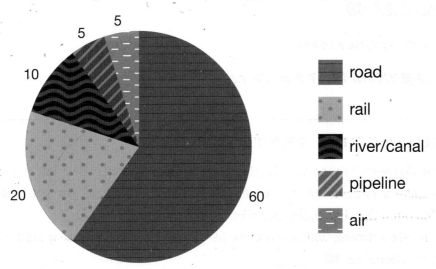

Modes of transport used to move goods between western region and rest of country (percentages)

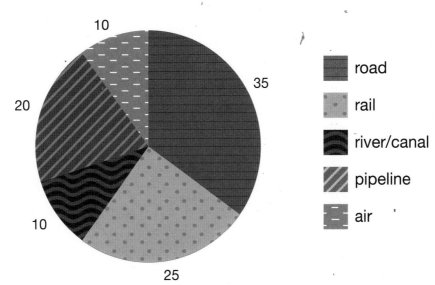

WRITING TASK 2

You should spend about 40 minutes on this task.

Write about the following topic:

> **In some countries, increasing numbers of people live alone.**
>
> **What do you think are the reasons for this? Do you think it is a positive or negative trend?**

Give reasons for your answer and include any relevant examples from your own knowledge or experience.

Write at least 250 words.

SPEAKING

PART 1 INTRODUCTION AND INTERVIEW

The examiner will introduce himself/herself and check your identification. Here is an example:

Can you tell me where you're from?
Can I see your identification, please?

The examiner will then ask some questions on familiar topics such as where you live, your work or studies, your family and your interests. Here are some examples:

Work/Study

• Do you work or are you a student?

Work

• What job do you do?
• How did you find this job?

PART 2 INDIVIDUAL LONG TURN

The examiner will give you a topic on a card and you have to talk about the topic for one or two minutes. You have one minute to think about what you want to say. You can make some notes to help you if you wish.

Here is an example of a candidate task card:

Eating and food

Describe a meal you enjoyed.

You should say:

    where you had the meal
    who was at the meal
    what you ate at the meal
and why you enjoyed the meal.

PART 3 DISCUSSION

The examiner will ask you some general questions which relate to the topic in Part 2. Here are some examples:

Eating and food

At which special times do families or friends eat a meal together in your country?
Do you agree or disagree that families should eat at least one meal together every day?
Explain how some kinds of food can damage your health.

Test 3

SECTION 1   Questions 1–10

Complete the notes below.

Write **NO MORE THAN TWO WORDS AND/OR A NUMBER** for each answer.

Cycling club notes

Example	Answer
James is the club	secretary

Membership:

○ chance for members to enter **1** ....

○ extra fee covers meetings with guest speakers and **2** ....

○ new members receive a free **3** .... for their bike

Practical information:

○ club meets in the village of **4** ....

○ tops with long sleeves and warmers for **5** .... available at a discount

○ payment for bike hire is on a **6** .... basis or per outing

Activities and events:

○ this summer's camping trip will be to the **7** ....

○ club runs a yearly **8** .... event for the local community

Contact details:

○ cycling shop telephone number: **9** ....

○ name of website: www.**10** ....com

SECTION 2   Questions 11–20

Questions 11–15

Complete the sentences below.

Write **NO MORE THAN TWO WORDS AND/OR A NUMBER** *for each answer.*

11 The speaker describes letter writing as a '........................'.

12 Writers used to use .... to exemplify their ideas.

13 Writers could talk about their .... in letters.

14 The speaker keeps her treasured letters in a ....

15 The speaker compares letters to a ....

Questions 16–20

Complete the notes below.

Write **ONE WORD ONLY** *for each answer.*

Tips for letter writing

- Find a **16** .... room.
- Avoid using **17** .... which may not last.
- Letters can act as a **18** .... (e.g. for seeking advice).
- Word every **19** .... carefully.
- Ensure you use an appropriate **20** ....

SECTION 3   *Questions 21–30*

Questions 21 and 22

*Choose **TWO** letters, **A–E**.*

Which **TWO** reasons do the students give for choosing the university they attend?

A   the opportunities to study abroad

B   the lower fees

C   the wide choice of courses offered

D   the location

E   the reputation of the teaching staff

Questions 23 and 24

*Choose **TWO** letters, **A–E**.*

Which **TWO** study groups are both students going to join?

A   grammar focus

B   conversation practice

C   writing skills

D   literature analysis

E   listening skills

Questions 25–30

*Write the correct letter, **A**, **B** or **C**, next to questions 25–30.*

Which problems do the students agree each online resource has?

Online Resources		Problems	
25 internet chat room	....	**A** operates too slowly	
26 translation software	....	**B** isn't accurate enough	
27 vocabulary builder	....	**C** has too few features	
28 online dictionary	....		
29 language lab	....		
30 writing checker	....		

SECTION 4   *Questions 31–40*

Complete the sentences below.

Write ONE WORD ONLY for each answer.

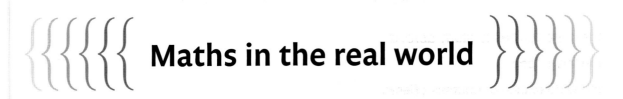

Maths in the real world

31   Students need .... and persistence to succeed in maths.

32   Students also have a need to understand the .... of the subject.

33   It is the teacher's role to make maths accessible. Maths is in everything we do, from using a .... to decorating a room.

34   Teachers should avoid using techniques involving .... or repetition.

35   People have applied similar .... for many generations.

36   Basic maths skills help us stick to a .... or understand trends.

37   Maths is essential in progressing our careers, much like .... skills.

38   It is also useful in hobbies like music or sailing. Students find it hard to see how maths relates to life outside school: studying risk assessment or .... makes this easier. Maths also helps us to find solutions to difficult life problems.

39   The way to study maths is to start from a .... of simple ideas and build up to more complex ones.

40   What teachers can do to help students see the point of maths: ask them to imagine life without calendars, watches, money or ....

READING PASSAGE 1

*You should spend about 20 minutes on **Questions 1–13**, which are based on Reading Passage 1 below.*

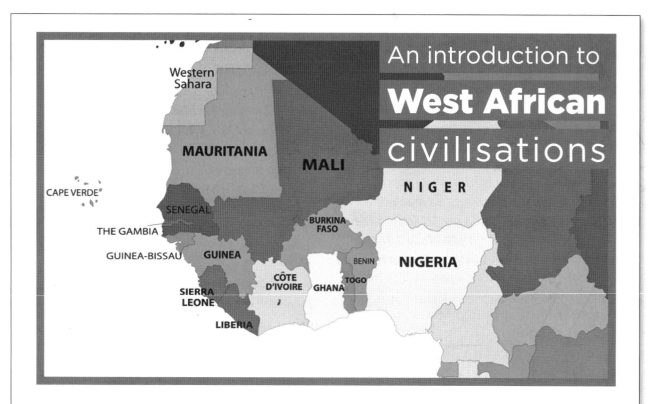

An introduction to **West African** civilisations

The West African region, as defined by the United Nations, consists of sixteen states, stretching from Mauritania, Mali and Niger in the north to the coastal countries of the south, such as Nigeria and Ghana. The Sahara Desert forms the northern boundary of the region, the Atlantic Ocean (including the Gulf of Guinea) the western and southern.

Around 8,000 years ago, towards the end of the Great Ice Age that affected much of the northern hemisphere, today's Sahara Desert was a productive environment providing enough food for a large settled population. However, as the climate changed, leading to desertification, many of its inhabitants migrated south to a more fertile region.

Key to the growth of West Africa over several thousand years was the domestication of cattle and camels and the development of ironworking technology. The production of iron tools and weapons contributed to improvements in agriculture, hunting and warfare, which in turn made towns sustainable. From the third century, if not earlier, camels were used for transport across the Sahara Desert, making it possible to trade with North Africa, the Middle East and Europe. Gold, metal ornaments, ivory, cotton cloth and other goods were exported in exchange for salt, horses, and manufactured goods such as textiles.

Trade and local resources led to prosperity, an effective system of taxation, centralised states and the development of larger urban centres. For example, by AD 500, Djenné-Djeno, on the River Niger, was a town of about 20,000 people, more than in most European towns of that time.

One of the earliest known cultures of the area was that of the Nok people, who lived in villages on a plateau in the centre of present-day Nigeria from around 1,000 BC. They appear to have had an advanced social system. Between 500 BC and AD 200 they created terracotta sculptures of human beings and animals, sometimes life-sized or a little smaller, the human heads often displaying jewellery and elaborate hairstyles. The statues were first discovered by chance in 1928, during tin-mining operations.

The function of the statues is uncertain: they may have been charms against crop failure, or were used to mark graves. Some appear to depict people suffering from particular diseases, giving rise to the suggestion that they were intended as charms against the illness in question. They vary so much it seems likely that each one was individually created, rather than being formed in a mould. The Nok also smelted and forged iron to make tools – at least by 550 BC, and possibly earlier.

Another technology used in West Africa to create figures – metal ones, in this case – is called lost-wax casting. It was common from around AD 900. In brief, the process begins with a piece of beeswax, which is carved into the desired shape, covered with several layers of clay, and heated. The wax melts, and is poured off, leaving only the clay shell. Then liquid gold, bronze or another metal is poured into this mould. When that has cooled and hardened, the clay shell is broken, to uncover the metal figure. The metals came from various sources: tin, for example, is plentiful in Nigeria, while brass was brought across the Sahara by Arab caravans from the twelfth century.

The Ghana, or Wagadou, Empire, probably arose in the eighth or ninth century, and lasted until the thirteenth. This state was located in part of modern Mauritania and Mali (it should not be confused with present-day Ghana, further to the east). The Empire's power and wealth were based on gold – a tenth-century Arab writer described Ghana as having the richest mines on earth. It benefited from the growth of trade across the Sahara when camels were introduced as a form of transport. Ghana seems to have been absorbed into the Mali Empire by the fourteenth century, though the reasons for this are disputed.

The Mali Empire expanded during the thirteenth and fourteenth centuries, developing into a centralised state covering much of West Africa. It gained a reputation for learning and prosperity. The city of Timbuktu, founded in the twelfth century, developed into a major educational centre. In 1324–5, the king, who had converted to Islam, undertook the traditional Muslim pilgrimage to Mecca, in modern Saudi Arabia. While breaking his journey in Egypt, his wealth and generosity created astonishment. He apparently gave away so much gold that its price collapsed, and did not recover for several years. A few decades later, the Moroccan traveller Ibn Battuta visited Mali, and was greatly impressed by the peaceful, law-abiding country. However, Mali fell into decline, and gradually came under the control of the Songhai.

From the fifteenth to the late sixteenth century, the Songhai controlled one of the largest Islamic empires in history. They are thought to have settled at Gao, on the Niger River in modern Mali, around the year 800, and established the state, with Gao as its capital, in the eleventh century. Its rise to regional domination began in 1464, when Sonni Ali Ber came to power and embarked on the conquest of much of the Mali Empire's territory, including Timbuktu and the important trading city of Djenné (a few kilometres from Djenné-Djeno, which had been abandoned by the thirteenth century). The Songhai Empire reached its peak in the sixteenth century under Sonni Ali's successors.

Questions 1–4

Do the following statements agree with the information given in Reading Passage 1?

In boxes 1–4 on your answer sheet, write

TRUE	*if the statement agrees with the information*
FALSE	*if the statement contradicts the information*
NOT GIVEN	*if there is no information on this*

1   The Sahara Desert produced plenty of food for its inhabitants about 8,000 years ago.

2   In AD 500, Djenné-Djeno was the largest town in Africa.

3   The Nok people's statues were discovered during archaeological excavations.

4   It is possible that Nok statues were made to protect people from disease.

Questions 5–9

Complete the flowchart below.

*Choose **ONE WORD ONLY** from the text for each answer.*

Write your answers in boxes 5–9 on your answer sheet.

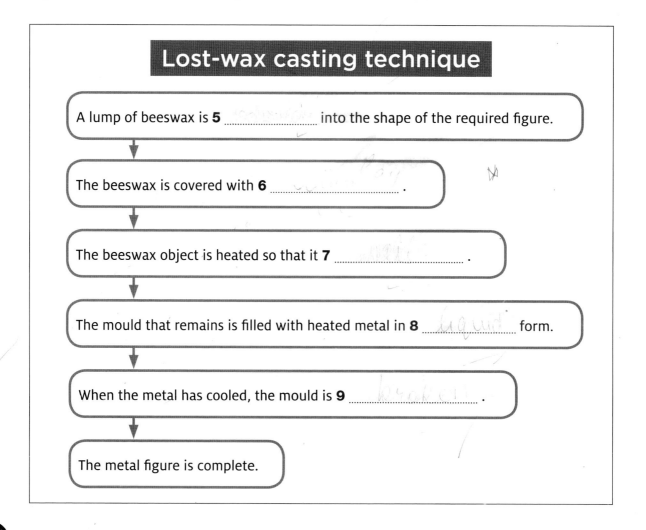

Lost-wax casting technique

A lump of beeswax is **5** _____ into the shape of the required figure.

↓

The beeswax is covered with **6** _____ .

↓

The beeswax object is heated so that it **7** _____ .

↓

The mould that remains is filled with heated metal in **8** _____ form.

↓

When the metal has cooled, the mould is **9** _____ .

↓

The metal figure is complete.

Questions 10–13

Complete the table below.

Choose **ONE WORD ONLY** from the text for each answer.

Write your answers in boxes 10–13 on your answer sheet.

Civilisation	Comment
Nok	known for statues made of **10** ....
Ghana Empire	wealth as a result of trade and the mining of **11** ....
Mali Empire	well known for wealth and **12** ....
Songhai Empire	increased power through **13** ....

READING PASSAGE 2

*You should spend about 20 minutes on **Questions 14–26**, which are based on Reading Passage 2 on pages 49 and 50.*

Questions 14–20

Reading Passage 2 has seven sections, **A–G**.

Choose the correct heading for each section from the list of headings below.

*Write the correct number, **i–ix**, in boxes 14–20 on your answer sheet.*

List of Headings

i	Climate change forced people to move to new areas
ii	The risk of overestimating the significance of volcanic ash layers
iii	The speed of climate change today may be nothing new
iv	A multi-disciplinary team
v	How volcanic ash is transported
vi	Why standard measurement techniques are less than ideal
vii	Identifying precise details of volcanic ash layers
viii	What material the scientists will analyse in a new approach to dating
ix	The downside of academic competitiveness

---

14 Section **A**

15 Section **B**

16 Section **C**

17 Section **D**

18 Section **E**

19 Section **F**

20 Section **G**

Abrupt climate change

Climate change taking place over a relatively short period is not a new phenomenon. A project is investigating such changes that occurred in the past.

A A research consortium, led by Professor John Lowe in the Geography Department at Royal Holloway, University of London, has been awarded funding of £3 million to develop a novel approach for assessing how humans may have responded to rapid environmental changes during the recent past. Among its tools, the team will use laser-based technology to provide a high degree of accuracy in dating. The five-year project is known as RESET (Response of Humans to Abrupt Environmental Transitions), and is funded by the Natural Environment Research Council. It brings together scientists from the Geography and Geology Departments of Royal Holloway, the University of Oxford, the Natural History Museum, London, and the University of Southampton, based at the National Oceanography Centre, Southampton. Together, they have expertise in human palaeontology, archaeology, oceanography, volcanic geology and past climate change.

B The driving forces behind major shifts in recent human evolution and adaptation have been the subject of intense debate for more than 100 years. The funding emphasises the importance of using records from the past to meet the challenge of climate change today. Ice-core records from Greenland have suggested that pronounced climatic shifts with severe environmental consequences have sometimes taken place within as little as 20 years or less. This means that some of our ancestors experienced climatic variability perhaps as rapid as those associated with global warming today.

C Our understanding of how humans responded to such abrupt events is limited however, largely because current studies are compromised by an inability to synchronise archaeological and geological records with sufficient precision. All geological dating methods are subject to some statistical uncertainty. Even in the case of radiocarbon dating, which is one of the most precise and flexible methods at scientists' disposal, age estimates can at best be narrowed down to a timespan of about a hundred years, and at worst, a few thousand. Most of the alternative dating methods are less flexible in their application and frequently produce results that are even less well constrained.

Professor John Lowe, scientific co-ordinator of RESET, explains, 'Being able to establish the precise temporal relationships between archaeological events and sudden changes in the environment has proved an elusive goal for scientists so far. Until this obstacle is overcome, answers to some of the most vital and intriguing questions about our recent past, and understanding fully their implications for the future, will remain tantalisingly beyond our grasp.'

D   The RESET project will construct a revised chronological framework for testing the hypothesis that major shifts in human development coincided with, or immediately followed, some prominent abrupt environmental transitions in the recent geological past. At the core of this framework are volcanic ash layers which are found in archaeological and geological records throughout Europe, and which were created at approximately the same time in widely separated locations.

E   Explosive volcanic eruptions generate large volumes of ash which are carried by air mass movements and the jet stream up to thousands of kilometres from the source volcano. Ash from Central Italy has been traced as far as Russia, and Icelandic ash regularly reaches Western Europe. A long history of explosions from Italian, Icelandic and other volcanic centres has led to a complex series of ash layers being laid down on the sea floor, in lakes, on peat-bogs, in archaeological sites, such as shallow caves, and even on to the Greenland ice cap.

F   Martin Menzies, Professor of Geochemistry at Royal Holloway, is leading one strand of the project concerning geochemical 'fingerprinting' of the ash layers. This strand (one of seven, in total) will provide the volcanic ash framework that underpins the project. Here the emphasis will be on maintaining and improving laboratory protocols for the detection, extraction and geochemical 'fingerprinting' of selected ash layers, for testing the chemical consistency of individual layers, and for refining their chronology. To achieve this, RESET will use laser-based technology to analyse key ash layers, producing a lattice that will tie together the various records, and bring greater clarity to the sequence of climatic and human events in Europe and North Africa during the last 80,000 years.

G   Professor Clive Gamble is leading the strand 'Re-populating Europe after the Last Glacial Stage'. With his colleagues he will focus on major archaeological events which occur during periods of abrupt environmental change, such as the movement north of hunters as climate rapidly changed from one of intense cold to conditions more similar to today. There is a rich archive of archaeological evidence which records the impact of these population movements, sometimes at a continental scale, and the team will develop new dating methods to assess their correspondence to the climate data.

Professor Chris Stringer, a specialist in human evolution, sums up, 'This project could take us into a new phase in the interdisciplinary study of prehistoric human development. Establishing the precise order of events is the key to resolving some of the long-standing debates about climate history and its impacts on the human dimension, and long-standing research questions such as the fate of the Neanderthals.'

Questions 21 and 22

Choose **TWO** letters, **A–E**.

Write the correct letters in boxes 21 and 22 on your answer sheet.

Which **TWO** of the following are among the goals of the RESET project?

A   to gain information that can help to deal with current climate change

B   to improve the accuracy of radiocarbon dating

C   to find previously unidentified layers of volcanic ash

D   to gain more information about population movements

E   to find out where Neanderthals lived

Questions 23–26

Look at the following descriptions (**Questions 23–26**) and the list of techniques below.

Match each description with the correct technique, **A, B** or **C**.

NB You may use any letter more than once.

Write the correct letter, **A, B** or **C** in boxes 23–26 on your answer sheet.

> **List of Techniques**
>
> **A**   use of ice-core records
>
> **B**   radiocarbon dating
>
> **C**   laser-based technology

23   suitable for calculating the relative dates of different ash layers   ....

24   cannot date an event to within less than a century   ....

25   has produced evidence that features of today's climate change are not new   ....

26   will increase understanding of the relationship between human and natural events   ....

READING PASSAGE 3

*You should spend about 20 minutes on **Questions 27–40**, which are based on Reading Passage 3 below.*

The
human brain

An introduction to a book about recent findings

The human brain has been slow to give up its secrets. Until relatively recently the machinations that give rise to our thoughts, memories, feelings and perceptions were impossible to examine directly – their nature could only be inferred by observing their effects. Now, however, new imaging techniques make the internal world of the mind visible, much as X-rays reveal our bones. Functional brain scanning machines are now opening up the territory of the mind just as the first ocean-going ships once opened up the globe.

The challenge of mapping this world – locating the precise brain activity that creates specific experiences and behavioural responses – is currently engaging some of the finest scientists in the world. This book brings news of their discoveries in a way that will make them comprehensible even to those with no knowledge of, or specific interest in, science.

Everyone should be enthralled by this venture because it is giving us greater understanding about one of the oldest and most fundamental of mysteries – the relationship between brain and mind. It is also providing fascinating insights into ourselves and shedding light on unusual and bizarre behaviour. The biological basis of mental illness, for example, is now demonstrable: no one can reasonably watch the frenzied, localised activity in the brain of a person driven by some obsession, or see the dull glow of a depressed brain, and still doubt that these are physical conditions rather than some sickness of the soul. Similarly, it is now possible to locate and observe the mechanics of rage, violence and misperception, and even to detect the physical signs of complex qualities of mind like kindness, humour, heartlessness, gregariousness, altruism, mother-love and self-awareness.

The knowledge that brain mapping is delivering is not only enlightening, it is of immense practical and social importance because it paves the way for us to recreate ourselves mentally in a way that has previously been described only in science fiction. Rather as knowledge of the human genome is enabling us to begin manipulating the fundamental physical processes that give rise to our bodies, so brain mapping is providing the navigational tool required to control brain activity in a precise and radical way.

Unlike genetic engineering, gaining this control does not depend on the development of tricky new technology – all it will take is a little refinement of existing methods and techniques like drugs, surgery, electrical and magnetic manipulation and psychological intervention. These are limited only in that, at present, they are (literally) hit-and-miss. When our brain maps are complete, however, it will be possible to target psychoactive treatments so finely that an individual's state of mind (and thus behaviour) will be almost entirely open to being changed. It may even be possible to alter individual perception to the extent that we could, if we chose, live in a state of virtual reality, almost entirely unaffected by the external environment.

This is an old ambition, of course, reflected in our perpetual attempts to alter our consciousness through sensation-seeking and trances. What is new is that brain mapping may soon make it possible without any of the usual drawbacks. The personal, social and political implications of this are awesome, and one of the most serious ethical questions we face in this century is deciding how this powerful new tool should be deployed.

Those who are actually engaged in brain mapping loathe this sort of talk. For people at the leading edge of scientific research, where findings are often hyped in the scramble for funding, they are oddly reticent about the potential uses of their work. One reason for this is that modern behavioural neuroscience is a new discipline and its practitioners have come into it from many different fields: physics, radiology, neurology, molecular biology, psychology and psychiatry – even mathematics and philosophy. They have yet to develop a group mentality or a commonly agreed purpose beyond their immediate task of charting brain function. Many neuroscientists are also terrified of what might happen if their work is ever subjected to the tabloid treatment that has been meted out to their opposite numbers in genetics. The Human Genome Project has led to endless apocalyptic headlines, and as a result the geneticists are now closely scrutinised and controlled. Brain researchers can do without that sort of attention.

The result of this reticence is that while we all debate and fret about the moral and practical implications of genetic engineering, brain mapping tends to be regarded as the geeks' corner of psychology – interesting, no doubt, for those who like that sort of thing, but of no practical importance. When news leaks out it tends to be in isolated blips: one tiny piece of brain tissue is found to be the source of fear; the connection between the two hemispheres appears to be denser in women than in men; damage is found in the frontal lobes of a disproportionate number of murderers on Death Row. Each of these stories generates a brief flurry of speculation, but their full significance is rarely elucidated.

Questions 27–31

*Choose the correct letter, **A**, **B**, **C** or **D**.*

Write the correct letter in boxes 27–31 on your answer sheet.

27 The writer refers to X-rays to make the point that

    A the study of the brain has been helped by developments in X-rays.

    B previously invisible brain activity can now be seen.

    C the study of bones is more advanced than the study of the brain.

    D it is now as easy to study the brain as it is to study bones.

28 What does the writer say about research into the brain in the second paragraph?

    A It is creating interest among many people who are not scientists.

    B Its findings have been under-reported among scientists.

    C It is changing generally held ideas about how the brain functions.

    D Its purpose is to link feelings and behaviour to what is happening in the brain.

29 In the third paragraph, the writer refers to 'the dull glow of a depressed brain' as evidence that mental illness

    A has physical causes.

    B is becoming more common.

    C brings about certain effects in the body.

    D can cause rage and violence.

30 The writer mentions science fiction in order to suggest that

    A research into the brain is stimulating the writing of science fiction.

    B it influences people's attitude towards brain mapping.

    C it has inspired scientists to carry out research into the brain.

    D some activities that were purely fictional will soon be real.

31 In the fourth paragraph, the writer claims that

    A certain objectives are still only achievable in science fiction.

    B genome research has influenced research into the brain.

    C it is becoming possible to make the brain do as we wish.

    D research is challenging certain ideas about the brain.

Questions 32–37

Do the following statements agree with the views of the writer in Reading Passage 3?

In boxes 32–37 on your answer sheet, write

YES	if the statement agrees with the views of the writer
NO	if the statement contradicts the views of the writer
NOT GIVEN	if it is impossible to say what the writer thinks about this

32 The book is targeted at readers with a scientific background.

33 Gaining control over the brain will require complicated new technology.

34 Maps of the brain will make it possible to alter specific aspects of people's behaviour.

35 It is desirable to reduce the impact on our lives of what is outside us.

36 Discussion about ethical issues is being influenced by governments.

37 The findings of scientific research are sometimes exaggerated in order to attract investment.

Questions 38–40

Complete each sentence with the correct ending, **A–F**, below.

Write the correct letter, **A–F** in boxes 38–40 on your answer sheet.

38 Behavioural neuroscientists do not want to discuss   ....

39 A number of behavioural neuroscientists wish to avoid   ....

40 The findings of behavioural neuroscience are usually treated as   ....

A	something of limited interest.
B	the kind of media coverage that geneticists receive.
C	an expectation that discoveries about the brain will be ignored.
D	potential applications that have proved disappointing.
E	the way that the results of their research should be used.
F	any way of attracting researchers from other fields.

ACADEMIC WRITING

WRITING TASK 1

You should spend about 20 minutes on this task.

> **The diagram below shows a process for making bricks.**
>
> **Summarise the information by selecting and reporting the main features, and make comparisons where relevant.**

Write at least 150 words.

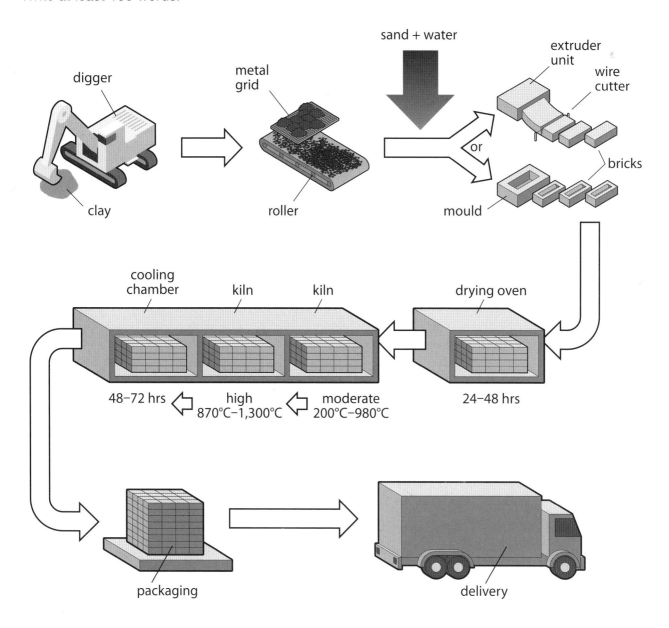

WRITING TASK 2

You should spend about 40 minutes on this task.

Write about the following topic:

> **Some people think that there is too much advertising in our daily lives.**
>
> **To what extent do you agree or disagree with this opinion?**

Give reasons for your answer and include any relevant examples from your own knowledge or experience.

Write at least 250 words.

PART 1   INTRODUCTION AND INTERVIEW

The examiner will introduce himself/herself and check your identification.

The examiner will then ask some questions on familiar topics such as where you live, your work or studies, your family and your interests. Here are some examples:

Work/Study

• Do you work or are you a student?

Study

• What subject or subjects do you study?
• What do you enjoy most about studying this subject / these subjects?

PART 2   INDIVIDUAL LONG TURN

The examiner will give you a topic on a card and you have to talk about the topic for one or two minutes. You have one minute to think about what you want to say. You can make some notes to help you if you wish.

Here is an example of a candidate task card:

Healthy activity

Describe an activity you have done to help you stay healthy.

You should say:

    which activity you have done
    why you did this activity
    how it made you feel
and how it has helped you stay healthy.

PART 3   DISCUSSION

The examiner will ask you some general questions which relate to the topic in Part 2. Here are some examples:

Healthy activity

What activities make people unhealthy?
Do you agree or disagree that young children have healthier lifestyles than teenagers?
How much do you think people's jobs affect how healthy they are?

Test 4

SECTION 1   Questions 1–10

Complete the form below.

Write **NO MORE THAN TWO WORDS AND/OR A NUMBER** for each answer.

SILVERTON HALL – Event Booking Form

Date and Time

Example	Answer
Date of event:	_15th January_

Day of week:	**1** ....
Room needed from:	7:30 p.m. until **2** ....

Event Details

Type of event:	**3** ....
Number of guests:	60 including some **4** .... guests
Catering requirements:	**5** .... and drinks
Equipment required:	**6** ....
Transport arrangements:	travel by **7** ....
Total cost:	**8** £ ....

Contact Details

Name:	Rob **9** ....
Phone:	**10** ....

SECTION 2   Questions 11–20

Questions 11–16

What comment does the manager make about each of the following steps in coffee processing?

*Choose **SIX** answers from the box and write the correct letter, **A–G**, next to questions 11–16.*

Description

A needs additional staff
B separates beans for different purposes
C is an unnecessary step
D is more expensive
E increases flavour
F is less polluting
G uses less space
H requires special skills

Steps in coffee processing

11	wet processing by machine	....
12	machine drying	....
13	natural drying	....
14	polishing	....
15	sorting by size	....
16	sorting by colour	....

Questions 17 and 18

*Choose **TWO** letters, **A–E**.*

Which **TWO** areas of the building are **not** part of the tour?

A the tasting room
B the shop
C the staff canteen
D the visitor centre
E the reception area

Questions 19 and 20

*Choose **TWO** letters, **A–E**.*

Which **TWO** things will each member of staff be provided with?

A protective shoes
B a name badge
C a cap
D gloves
E pen and notebook

SECTION 3   Questions 21–30

Questions 21–26

*Choose the correct letter, **A**, **B** or **C**.*

21 What gave Tim the idea for his dissertation proposal?

   A   His grandmother asked him to record her language.

   B   He heard about a linguistic project he wanted to join.

   C   He learned about conserving languages on his course.

22 When talking about the impact of technology, Tim

   A   points out a problem caused by its spread.

   B   explains how it can be used to conserve language.

   C   emphasises its importance for communication.

23 Tim and his tutor decide that in the introduction to his dissertation, he should discuss

   A   the impact of the media on language.

   B   how globalisation has helped remote communities.

   C   the reasons why he talks to his grandmother in English.

24 What does Tim say about documenting dying languages?

   A   He believes writing a language down stops it from falling out of use.

   B   He sees little point in trying to revive languages that are already dead.

   C   He is unconvinced that his grandmother's language can be saved.

25 Tim's tutor explains to him that recording minority languages is

   A   something that schoolchildren can be involved in.

   B   a way to allow future generations to experience them.

   C   a useful tool for training language teachers.

26 When talking about language and culture, Tim

   A   highlights why family traditions are important to him.

   B   describes how the two subjects are linked together.

   C   expresses a desire to learn about his family's customs.

Questions 27 and 28

*Choose **TWO** letters, **A–E**.*

Which **TWO** areas of language does the tutor recommend Tim to focus on?

A   written language

B   context of speech

C   translations of written samples

D   vocabulary items

E   grammar points

Questions 29 and 30

*Choose **TWO** letters, **A–E**.*

Which **TWO** approaches to recording do Tim and his tutor decide he should take?

A   covering as much as possible

B   doing several recording sessions

C   keeping a record of times and places

D   writing things down immediately

E   waiting a few days before listening back to it

SECTION 4   Questions 31–40

Questions 31–33

*Choose the correct letter **A**, **B** or **C**.*

31 Humans first started tracking time

    A 30,000 years ago.

    B 25,000 years ago.

    C 5,000 years ago.

32 Horizon tracking involved recording

    A where the sun rose and set.

    B the times of sunrise and sunset.

    C the length of the shortest day.

33 Time measurement improved when

    A trees were planted on hill-tops.

    B special constructions were erected.

    C people began living in larger groups.

Questions 34–36

Complete the sentences below.

*Write **ONE WORD ONLY** for each answer.*

34 The first clocks worked by making a small hole in a .... and allowing water to drip out.

35 Sundials measured time by noting where the sun's shadow fell on the .... marked on the dial.

36 Workers in China and Japan changed activities when the .... of the incense changed.

Questions 37–40

Answer the questions below.

*Write **NO MORE THAN TWO WORDS AND/OR A NUMBER** for each question.*

37 What object made the wheels of a mechanical clock go round?

38 What invention created a problem with communities having different times?

39 In which year was a time system for England nationally agreed?

40 Which building in Greenwich was chosen as the point from which to measure time?

READING PASSAGE 1

*You should spend about 20 minutes on **Questions 1–13**, which are based on Reading Passage 1 below.*

THE PHAROS LIGHTHOUSE AT ALEXANDRIA

One of the Seven Wonders of the Ancient World

The story of the Pharos lighthouse starts with the founding of the city of Alexandria by the Macedonian conqueror Alexander the Great in 332 BC. Alexander founded at least seventeen cities named Alexandria at different locations in his vast domain. Most of them disappeared, but Alexandria in Egypt thrived for many centuries and is still prosperous today.

Alexander the Great chose the location of his new city on the Mediterranean Sea carefully. Instead of building it on the Nile delta, he selected a site some twenty miles to the west, so that the silt and mud carried by the river would not block the city harbour. Another reason was that the marshy Lake Mareotis was situated south of the city and so after a canal was constructed between the lake and the River Nile, the city had more than one port: one for Nile traffic, and the other for Mediterranean Sea trade.

Alexander died in 323 BC and the city was completed by Ptolemy Soter, the new ruler of Egypt. Under Ptolemy the city became rich and prosperous. However, it was felt to need both a landmark and a mechanism to guide the many trade ships into its busy harbour. Ptolemy authorised the building of the Pharos in 290 BC, and when it was completed some twenty years later, it was the first lighthouse in the world and the tallest building in existence, with the exception of the Great Pyramid. The construction cost was said to have been 800 talents, an amount equal today to about three million dollars.

Construction of the Lighthouse

The lighthouse's designer is believed to have been Sostratus of Knidos, though some sources argue he only provided the financing for the project. Proud of his work, Sostratus desired to have his name carved into the foundation. Ptolemy II, the son who ruled Egypt after his father, refused this request, wanting only his own name to be on the building. A clever man, Sostratus supposedly had the inscription

SOSTRATUS SON OF DEXIPHANES OF KNIDOS ON BEHALF OF ALL MARINERS TO THE SAVIOR GODS

chiselled into the foundation, then covered it with plaster. Into the plaster was carved Ptolemy's name. As the years went by (and after the death of both Sostratus and Ptolemy) the plaster aged and chipped away, revealing Sostratus's dedication.

The lighthouse was built on the island of Pharos and soon the building itself acquired that name. The connection of the name with the function became so strong that the word 'pharos' became the root of the word meaning 'lighthouse' in French, Italian, Spanish and Romanian.

There are two detailed descriptions made of the lighthouse in the tenth century AD. According to these accounts, the building was 300 cubits high which is about 450 feet (140 m).

The design was unlike the slim, single column of most modern lighthouses, but more like the structure of an early twentieth-century skyscraper. There were three sections, one on top of another. The building material was stone, faced with white marble blocks cemented together with lead mortar. The lowest level of the building, which sat on a high stone platform, was shaped like a massive box. The entrance to this section of the building was not at the bottom of the structure, but part way up and reached by a long ramp. On top of that first section was an eight-sided tower. The final section on top of the tower was a cylinder, covered by an open cupola, where the fire that provided the light burned. On the roof was a large statue, probably of the god of the sea, Poseidon.

The interior had a shaft with a system of ropes that was used to transport fuel up to the fire. Staircases allowed visitors and the keepers to climb to the beacon at the top of the cylindrical section. There, according to reports, a large curved mirror, perhaps made of polished bronze, was used to project the fire's light into a beam. It was said ships could detect the light from the Pharos at night, or the smoke from the fire during the day, up to 100 miles away.

The lighthouse was apparently a tourist attraction from the start. Food was sold to visitors on the observation platform at the top of the first level. A smaller balcony provided an outlook from the top of the eight-sided tower for those who wanted to make the additional climb. The view from there must have been impressive as there were few places in the ancient world where a person could ascend a man-made tower to get such a perspective.

Destruction of the Lighthouse

Most accounts indicate that the Pharos stood for over 1,500 years, apparently surviving a tsunami that hit the eastern Mediterranean in 365 AD with minor damage. After that, however, tremors might have been responsible for cracks that appeared in the structure at the end of the tenth century and required a restoration that lowered the height of the building by about 70 feet. Then in 1303 AD, a major earthquake shook the region and put the Pharos permanently out of action, though ruins remained on the site for some time until 1480 when they were moved to construct a fortress on the island that still stands today.

Questions 1–6

Do the following statements agree with the information given in Reading Passage 1?

In boxes 1–6 on your answer sheet, write

TRUE	*if the statement agrees with the information*
FALSE	*if the statement contradicts the information*
NOT GIVEN	*if there is no information on this*

1   The city of Alexandria in Egypt was the most beautiful of Alexander the Great's cities.

2   A canal was built to prevent the harbour being blocked by mud and salt.

3   The site of Alexandria was chosen because it meant the city could have two harbours.

4   When the Pharos was built, it was the tallest building in the world.

5   Ptolemy II was initially unhappy with Sostratus's design for the Pharos.

6   Sostratus's plan was for his name to be visible to future generations.

Questions 7–9

Label the diagram below.

Choose **ONE WORD ONLY** from the passage for each answer.

Write your answers in boxes 7–9 on your answer sheet.

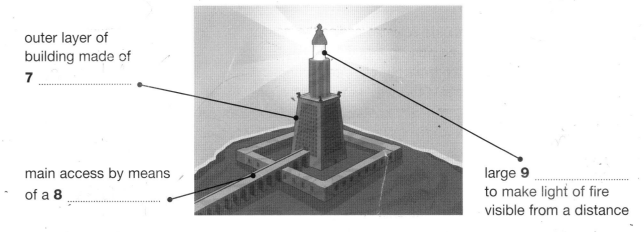

outer layer of
building made of
7 ....

main access by means
of a **8** ....

large **9** ....
to make light of fire
visible from a distance

Questions 10–13

Answer the questions below.

Choose **ONE WORD ONLY** from the passage for each answer.

Write your answers in boxes 10–13 on your answer sheet.

10   What did people use to lift wood to the top of the Pharos?

11   What could people buy when they went to visit the Pharos?

12   What caused the Pharos to collapse?

13   What building was some of the stone from the Pharos used for?

READING PASSAGE 2

*You should spend about 20 minutes on **Questions 14–26**, which are based on Reading Passage 2 below.*

Worms, water and Bollywood

An Indian agricultural research institution has developed a series of simple technologies to improve the productivity of small farms across the developing world.

Alina Paul reports.

A Water and fertile soil are essential for farmers everywhere, but in much of the developing world, one or both is often in short supply. For this reason, many development agencies are concentrating their efforts on ways to improve water access and soil fertility for rural families, with some notable successes. Based in Hyderabad, in Andhra Pradesh, India, the International Crops Research Institute for the Semi-Arid Tropics (ICRISAT) is a non-profit group that conducts agricultural research for development in Asia and sub-Saharan Africa, primarily working on drought-tolerant crops and sustainable land-management systems.

B Suhas Wani, the principal scientist leading the institute's watershed-management programme, has been working with the Indian government, local non-governmental organisations (NGOs), farm research centres and, most importantly, the smallholders themselves for the past 30 years. His work has shown that an integrated approach that takes in everything from building dams and conserving rainwater to providing training on vermicomposting* and strengthening women's self-help groups, can have a significant impact on crop yields and, consequently, household incomes. Wani's research on micronutrient addition to smallholder fields has provided benefits for some 3.5 million families in India. 'While many know about the need for phosphate and nitrogen, few realise the importance of micronutrients such as zinc and boron for plant growth,' he explains. 'We train local farm centres to analyse the soil samples so that smallholders can manage their soil health in the long term.'

C Niruji, who has a smallholding in the nearby village of Sharam, has benefited considerably from the work of ICRISAT. 'I sent a soil sample to the local farm-support centre, where it was tested. They explained to me that the sample was lacking in many things, such as zinc, boron and sulphur,' she continues. 'They helped me to get these ingredients and now not only does my turmeric mature faster, I also get much more yield.' Niruji also increased her access to water when she used a self-help group to get a loan for equipment to dig her well deeper. She now rents this out at 300 rupees (£3.75) a day, bringing her a good additional income. With the extra water, she's also just started to grow green fodder, which she sells locally. The fodder is used to feed buffalo, whose milk is then sold to a dairy cooperative.

D   In Kothapally, a drought-prone village in Andhra Pradesh, water scarcity once meant that families migrated to the city during the dry season and poverty was widespread. Today, Kothapally is prosperous, boasting healthy crop yields, even in the baking summer. The difference is largely down to a thirteen-year watershed-management project run by ICRISAT and its partners. The community's 270 farmer families all became members of a watershed association, which received assistance from scientists to identify and build water-harvesting structures and recharge groundwater. The Kothapally project proved so successful that it is now being replicated in China, Thailand and Vietnam.

E   Only four per cent of cropland in sub-Saharan Africa is irrigated. Farmers in the region grow rain-fed staple crops such as millet during the three-to-six-month rainy season, but rainfall variability is high, and typically crops fail twice every five years. By guaranteeing a water supply, micro-irrigation can reduce the risk that the harvest will fail and offer the possibility of a second harvest, while also opening up the option of growing high-value vegetables or fruits for sale. Growing a variety of nutrient-rich crops also adds diversity to the farmer's diet. Developed by ICRISAT and the World Vegetable Centre, the African Market Garden (AMG) is an approach to vegetable production that uses a small-scale, low-pressure, drip-irrigation system. Adding just enough water to the soil, drop by drop, around the roots of the plants cuts wastage by up to 80 per cent. With this precise irrigation, there are also fewer pests, meaning less labour, fertiliser and pesticide use.

F   In West Africa, most women have no or few rights to agricultural land, so ICRISAT has been working with local NGOs to encourage women to form associations and gain access to communal village wasteland. The women's groups are then trained to farm this degraded soil. 'It's not just about growing our own food,' says 35-year-old Oumou, who lives in Sadoré village in Niger. Four years ago, Oumou became the president of the Sadoré women's association and started farming on the village wasteland. Since then, she has been producing okra, hibiscus and sesame, some of which are sold and the remainder consumed by her family. 'All of the women in our association now have a right to this land,' says Oumou. 'We receive income from the produce we sell so we are less dependent on our husbands and more respected in the village.'

G   The key question remains how to scale up these successful examples of poverty reduction to increase their impact. One potential answer can be found in India, with the work of the NGO, International Development Enterprises India (IDEI). One of IDEI's most remarkable innovations isn't technological – it's the way it mass markets its ideas and equipment to remote, poorly educated rural communities. IDEI's video van travels from village to village screening Bollywood-style films that feature the treadle pump and drip irrigation, set within a typical mix of drama, romance and a happy ending. The films are tailored to each region, using well-known local actors to portray small farmers who escape poverty, thanks to simple, affordable technology. The open-air screenings in village squares attract the farmers' initial interest and IDEI's local team then follows up on that interest the next day.

* a system in which organic waste is placed in a pit and worms are added to make compost

Questions 14–18

Reading Passage 2 has seven paragraphs, **A–G**.

Which paragraph contains the following information?

Write the correct letter, **A–G**, in boxes 14–18 on your answer sheet.

14   a reference to the ownership of farming land being restricted

15   details of an initiative that is being adopted in several other countries

16   an explanation of why various organisations have a particular focus

17   the consequences of a reduced number of insects damaging crops

18   a solution to many farmers having limited knowledge of soil composition

Questions 19–22

Complete the summary below.

Choose **ONE WORD ONLY** from the passage for each answer.

Write your answers in boxes 19–22 on your answer sheet.

Farmers in the villages of Sharam and Kothapally

Niruji, who has a small farm in Sharam in India, has received help to improve the quality of the soil and as a result the **19** .... that she has always grown there produces a better harvest. She has also been able to introduce another crop, which is then sold and given to **20** ....

In the village of Kothapally, ICRISAT has arranged for **21** .... to show farmers how to improve water supplies. Crop yields are now higher, including during the **22** .... which has led to an increase in the incomes of the farmers.

Questions 23 and 24

Choose **TWO** letters **A–E**.

Write the correct letters in boxes 23 and 24 on your answer sheet.

The list below describes situations that affect farmers.

Which **TWO** are mentioned by the writer of the text in connection with farming in sub-Saharan Africa?

A   Crops are often damaged due to unpredictable weather patterns.

B   Farmers have to travel a long way to take the vegetables they have grown to market.

C   Improved water provision can mean that farmers have a wider range of foods to eat.

D   The cost of fertiliser has risen beyond the means of many farmers.

E   The irrigation systems that are in use require a constant source of water.

Questions 25 and 26

*Choose **TWO** letters **A–E**.*

Write the correct letters in boxes 25 and 26 on your answer sheet.

Which **TWO** of the following statements about farming communities in West Africa are made by the writer?

A   Women's groups in some communities are cultivating crops that are not typical to the area.

B   Organisations have helped members of the community to farm previously uncultivated land.

C   In some communities there is pressure to change the law regarding ownership of land.

D   There has been opposition in some communities to the formation of women's groups.

E   A recent initiative has improved the status of some members of the community.

READING PASSAGE 3

*You should spend about 20 minutes on **Questions 27–40**, which are based on Reading Passage 3 below.*

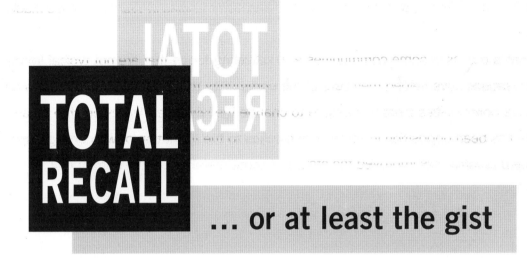

TOTAL RECALL ... or at least the gist

Our memory is like an ear of corn. At least, that's what Valerie Reyna was taught in graduate school. Its simple, homey feel notwithstanding, the metaphor seemed scientifically sound. After all, researchers had already concluded there were two distinct types of memory: *verbatim*, which allows us to recall what specifically happened at any given moment, and gist, which enables us to put the event in context and give it meaning. 'We were taught you extracted the gist from the verbatim memory,' recalled Reyna, an experimental psychologist and former senior research adviser to the US Department of Education. 'It was like husking an ear of corn. You threw away the husk, which was the verbatim, and you kept the gist, which was the kernel of meaning.' There it was: Neat. Simple. And also, as Reyna discovered over decades of subsequent research, wrong.

After conducting numerous studies with her partner, psychologist Charles Brainerd, Reyna concluded that verbatim and gist memory are separate, parallel systems. So separate, in fact, that 'there is some evidence' they occupy different sections of the brain. Reyna and Brainerd's hypothesis, which they call 'fuzzy trace theory', explains how we can 'remember' things that never really happened.

When an event occurs, verbatim memory records an accurate representation. But even as it is doing so, gist memory begins processing the data and determining how it fits into our existing storehouse of knowledge. Verbatim memories generally die away within a day or two, leaving only the gist memory, which records the event as we interpreted it. Under certain circumstances, this can produce a phenomenon Reyna and her colleagues refer to as 'phantom recollection'. She calls this 'a powerful form of false alarm' in which gist memory – designed to look for patterns and fill in perceived gaps – creates a vivid but illusory image (the phantom recollection) in our mind. Mental snapshots soon fade; what linger are our impressions of an occurrence, which are shaped by the meanings we attach to it. Reyna explains that people think they are recalling something accurately, but they are not.

Reyna and Brainerd, both professors in the department of human development at Cornell University in the US, summarised the research in this arena in their 2005 book *The Science of False Memory*. It spawned a series of follow-up studies, some of which are ongoing. 'We're looking at a number of things, including the effect of emotion on memory – how emotion interacts with your interpretation of events,' Reyna said. 'Does excitement interfere with your encoding of memory? Does it "stamp it in", as some of the neuroscience literature suggests? The effect might be more complex than that.'

One question that cannot be answered in the lab is why, in evolutionary terms, we would develop two separate memory systems. Reyna, who has given this considerable thought, noted that if all we had was our rapidly fading verbatim memory, 'it would be very hard to function, especially in an oral culture.' Consider the case of one of our prehistoric ancestors who is attacked by a sabre-toothed tiger. Verbatim memory would tell him precisely where the attack took place, exactly what the tiger looked like and what tree he climbed to get beyond the animal's reach. Gist memory would tell him: 'Tigers are dangerous. I'd better bring my spear,' The first would be interesting; the second, essential.

So gist memory allows us to make snap decisions based on 'fuzzy' representations of the past. But life does not always follow familiar patterns, and harm can result when we discard evidence that does not fit our assumptions.

False memories arguably do the most damage in courtrooms, where jurors often consider eyewitness testimony particularly convincing evidence. The good news is there are clues that indicate whether a witness is remembering a situation accurately. 'There are things you can look for,' Reyna said. 'There are circumstances that lend themselves more to accurate testimony', such as actually visiting the scene of the crime. 'To their immense credit, the courts are very open to the science,' she added. 'We have a long way to go, but we're moving in [a positive] direction. I recently wrote a chapter of a handbook for lawyers. Several of my colleagues told me, "You'll have to dumb that down." But the reaction was exactly the opposite. Lawyers wanted to read the original article and learn about the methodology.'

One of Reyna and Brainerd's most controversial courtroom-related findings was released last year. It suggested the testimony of children might be more accurate than that of adults. This belief was supported by an experiment in which they presented lists of words to groups of first-, fifth- and ninth-graders. Most, but not all, of the words were grouped by subject matter. After a short break, the children were given new lists of words belonging to the same subjects and asked to identify which were repeats. Consistently, the older children had more false memories, checking off words they thought they had seen earlier, but in fact had not.

Reyna was not surprised by these results. She noted that young children are forced to rely on verbatim memory, since their gist memory is still in its formative stage. Reyna cautioned, however, that many factors are involved when it comes to court testimony by youngsters. While their memories may indeed play fewer tricks on them, 'Kids are much more susceptible to suggestibility from social factors,' she said. In other words, they may feel compelled to say what a trusted adult wants or expects them to say.

Questions 27–29

*Choose the correct letter, **A**, **B**, **C** or **D**.*

Write the correct letter in boxes 27–29 on your answer sheet.

27 The term 'phantom recollection' refers to circumstances when

    A people's fear makes them recall an event more intensely.

    B people's memory is coloured by what they feel about an event.

    C verbatim memory remains for longer but in an incomplete state.

    D people remember something that is linked to an imaginary story.

28 Reyna tells a story about a prehistoric man in order to point out

    A why gist memory is necessary for survival.

    B how memory evolved over thousands of years.

    C the importance of passing memories on to others.

    D the value of verbatim memory in recognising threats.

29 When referring to the effects of memory in law courts, Reyna reveals her

    A satisfaction at the legal professionals' attitude to her research.

    B surprise at some witnesses' ability to remember the past.

    C interest in particular aspects of solving difficult crimes.

    D concern at the frequent failures of the jury system.

Questions 30–34

*Complete the summary using the list of words, **A–I**, below.*

*Write the correct letter, **A–I**, in boxes 30–34 on your answer sheet.*

Reyna and Brainerd's research into child witnesses

Results pointed to the possibility that, compared to more mature witnesses, children's evidence would be more trustworthy. The researchers gave schoolchildren words mainly arranged in lists relating to various **30** .... Having let them relax for a while, they handed out more lists, asking them to note if there were any **31** .... with the previous lists. Interestingly, the **32** .... increased with the age of the subjects. Reyna explained that **33** .... in the very young is still developing. She also noted, however, that children can be open to the **34** .... of others, and thus change what they report in their witness statements.

A	verbatim memory	**B**	sections	**C**	matches
D	topics	**E**	influence	**F**	gist memory
G	comparisons	**H**	errors	**I**	supervision

Questions 35–40

Do the following statements agree with the claims of the writer in Reading Passage 3?

In boxes 35–40 on your answer sheet, write

YES	*if the statement agrees with the claims of the writer*
NO	*if the statement contradicts the claims of the writer*
NOT GIVEN	*if it is impossible to say what the writer thinks about this*

35 After considerable research, Reyna and Brainerd decided that gist memory is totally detached from verbatim memory.

36 Fuzzy trace theory describes a phenomenon that Reyna and Brainerd have experienced.

37 Gist memory only starts working on the data from a past occurrence once verbatim memory has finished recording it.

38 Verbatim memory fades more rapidly as people age.

39 In Reyna's opinion, the neuroscience theory that strong emotion can fix a memory might be too simplistic.

40 Gist memory forces us to take time to reach a decision.

ACADEMIC WRITING

WRITING TASK 1

You should spend about 20 minutes on this task.

> *The chart below shows the total sales value by product category in one particular store, in a three-year period.*
>
> *Summarise the information by selecting and reporting the main features, and make comparisons where relevant.*

Write at least 150 words.

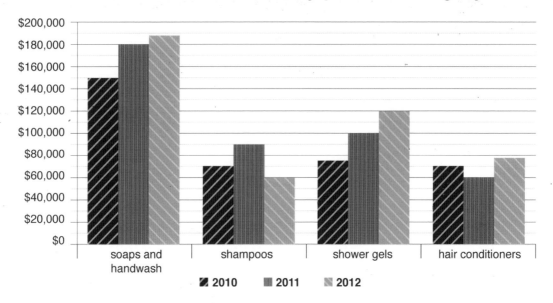

WRITING TASK 2

You should spend about 40 minutes on this task.

Write about the following topic:

> *Physical exercise is important for health, but some people do very little exercise.*
>
> *What are the effects of doing very little exercise? How can people be encouraged to do more exercise?*

Give reasons for your answer and include any relevant examples from your own knowledge or experience.

Write at least 250 words.

SPEAKING

PART 1   INTRODUCTION AND INTERVIEW

The examiner will introduce himself/herself and check your identification.

The examiner will then ask some questions on familiar topics such as where you live, your work or studies, your family and your interests. Here are some examples:

Public transport

- Do you like using public transport, for example, buses and trains? [Why? / Why not?]
- What kinds of public transport are available in your town/city?

PART 2   INDIVIDUAL LONG TURN

The examiner will give you a topic on a card and you have to talk about the topic for one or two minutes. You have one minute to think about what you want to say. You can make some notes to help you if you wish.

Here is an example of a candidate task card:

> ### Having a good time
>
> Describe an event, for example, a party, a festival or a celebration, that made you feel happy.
>
> You should say:
>
>   what the event was
>   when the event was
>   what happened at the event
> and why it made you feel happy.

PART 3   DISCUSSION

The examiner will ask you some general questions which relate to the topic in Part 2. Here are some examples:

Having a good time

What kind of activities do most people do to have a good time?
How does the way we have a good time change as we get older?
Would you like to spend your whole life just having a good time? [Why? / Why not?]

General Training Test 1

SECTION 1   Questions 1–14

Read the text below and answer Questions 1–8.

Some of London's less well-known museums

A   Open seven days a week, the **London Transport Museum** demonstrates how buses and trains have transformed the daily lives of both residents and visitors since the early nineteenth century. It includes a traditional red double-decker bus and the world's first steam train that ran underground – as long ago as 1863. It also traces developments in mapping the Underground and the evolution of the London Transport logo.

B   The nineteenth-century engineers Marc Isambard Brunel and his son Isambard Kingdom Brunel designed and constructed the Thames Tunnel, the first ever tunnel under a river. The **Brunel Museum** is located in the engine house, where pumps (no longer there) were installed to keep the tunnel dry. The exhibition tells the story of the construction and history of the pedestrian tunnel, which now forms part of the London railway network. The museum is open every day of the week.

C   The 3,500 fans in the **Fan Museum** represent a period of a thousand years and come from around the world; the museum places them in their historical, sociological and economic contexts. They have served as cooling devices, ceremonial tools, fashion accessories, status symbols, commemorative presents and advertising giveaways. The museum will also take orders for fans to be created in its workshops to match your requirements.

D   **Dennis Severs' House** has been restored to what it was in the early eighteenth century. It is lit by candles and fires, there is a smell of food being cooked, and sounds from the eighteenth-century street are audible. It seems the occupants will return at any moment. The museum is open on Sunday afternoons and Monday lunchtimes. For a truly magical experience, special 'Silent Night' visits are arranged one or two evenings a week, which must be booked in advance.

E   The main exhibit in the **Kirkaldy Testing Museum** is the 'All Purpose Testing Machine', designed by the nineteenth-century Scottish engineer David Kirkaldy and still in the laboratory that Kirkaldy built for it. It was designed to test the strength of materials such as bricks, concrete, iron and steel, and made a major contribution to the development of modern material science and mechanical engineering.

Questions 1–8

The text on page 78 has five sections, **A–E**.

For which museum are the following statements true?

*Write the correct letters, **A–E**, in boxes 1–8 on your answer sheet.*

NB *You may use any letter more than once.*

1 This museum is open on a limited number of days each week.

2 This museum is in a building that originally contained machinery for removing water.

3 The exhibits in this museum include vehicles that were used by the public.

4 This museum provides information about a structure that is now part of a different transport system.

5 This museum contains equipment in its original location.

6 You can arrange to have something made for you at this museum.

7 Some exhibits in this museum show changes in the way a railway system is represented.

8 This museum is designed to appeal to several senses.

Part-time leisure courses at Whitterham College

Whitterham College has an excellent reputation for its full-time Higher Education courses – designed for people just starting out on their career path or wanting to go to university – and for its part-time courses.

The numerous part-time evening and weekend leisure courses range from sculpture to sailing, foreign languages to forestry. Courses vary in length: some are intensive, two-day sessions, while at the opposite extreme, others last for an hour a week throughout the college year. Each intensive course is offered two or three times during the college year. Please note that for some courses, the fee includes the use of particular equipment or materials.

Our aim is to run courses as advertised, but if insufficient people enrol for a particular course, we will have to cancel it. If this happens, we will give you the choice of an appropriate alternative or your money back in full. A course may also be cancelled if it starts and the number of people attending falls below a certain level. In this case, a partial refund will be made.

Leisure courses are a great way to meet people with a similar interest and to develop a hobby – maybe even to gain the knowledge you need to turn it into a career. Several of our tutors are well-known in their fields, and you will be able to benefit from their experience.

The minimum age for enrolment on an adult leisure course is sixteen – we also offer classes to children under the age of sixteen.

College facilities, including the café and learning centre, are open to participants in leisure courses during the evening and weekend. Unfortunately, to prevent overcrowding, they are restricted to full-time students until 5 p.m. on weekdays.

Questions 9–14

Do the following statements agree with the information given in the text on page 80?

In boxes 9–14 on your answer sheet, write

TRUE	*if the statement agrees with the information*
FALSE	*if the statement contradicts the information*
NOT GIVEN	*if there is no information on this*

9   Intensive courses are repeated more than once.

10 A minimum number of participants are required for a course to run.

11 If the college cancels a course after it has started, participants will be given their money back in full.

12 Some past students have become tutors on the courses.

13 Some courses are especially for children with their parents.

14 Participants in leisure courses can use the learning centre whenever it is open.

Read the text below and answer Questions 15–20.

TO ALL STAFF: **WORKPLACE TRAINING**

The recent merger between Atkinson Dowell and RVP Motors that led to the formation of ADR Motors has presented an excellent opportunity to assess the training provided by each of the former companies. As training manager, I have carried out this evaluation with the assistance of colleagues, and we have formulated a plan for a unified system of training.

One aim is to maximise the company's competitiveness: over recent years both companies lost market share and we intend to reverse this trend within the next year. In addition, we will make strenuous efforts to improve staff satisfaction and reduce turnover, which in the case of Atkinson Dowell had reached an unacceptable level.

Following consultation with staff representatives, we are now in the process of setting up a training programme to meet the needs and interests of all employees. Here is some background information.

We have carried out an audit of the company's current job functions, the skills that they require and those already possessed by workers. We also invited all staff to fill in a survey, to identify the skills they wish to develop, both for their existing jobs and for the future. Over 50 per cent were returned, providing useful information about staff needs and interests.

As well as assessing the needs of existing staff, we have analysed our recruitment process and induction for new staff. As a result, we are now revising the person specifications relating to each position, to ensure that essential and desirable characteristics accurately reflect up-to-date job specifications, given that the nature of certain positions has changed.

As our existing in-house training resources are very limited, the training will largely be supplied by external providers. We are in contact with a number of organisations, to find the most suitable training for different skills. We expect that, in most cases, employees will need to attend courses on premises provided by the training organisation.

Your department manager will discuss your training needs with you individually before the end of next month, and a detailed training programme will then be planned.

Questions 15–20

Complete the sentences below.

*Choose **ONE WORD ONLY** from the text for each answer.*

Write your answers in boxes 15–20 on your answer sheet.

15 ADR Motors has been formed as the result of a ....

16 The company will try hard to lower the high .... of staff.

17 The company has carried out a .... exercise about training with representatives of its employees.

18 Employees were asked to complete a .... about their training needs.

19 The company has examined the .... programme arranged for newly-employed staff.

20 Most of the company's training needs will be met by .... training organisations.

Read the text below and answer Questions 21–27.

PRINCIPAL STATEMENT OF TERMS AND CONDITIONS

This statement is issued by Mather Electronics Ltd. It sets out your terms and conditions and forms part of your Contract of Employment. You will be notified in writing within one month of any change.

1   Your employment with us began on 1 April 2013.

2   You are employed as a Marketing Assistant. Your duties are as outlined in your job description.

3   Your normal place of work will be the Company's Head Office. However, the Company reserves the right, after appropriate consultation with you, to change your base should the needs of the Company require this.

4   Your working hours will be 37.5 hours per week, from 9 a.m. until 5.30 p.m., Monday to Friday, inclusive of one hour's lunch break each day. If the Company requires you to work any hours in addition to this, on a temporary basis, overtime payments will be made in line with the Company Remuneration Policy.

5   The current annual salary for this post is £22,500. This will be reviewed annually. You are also eligible for bonuses based on team performance as outlined in the Company Remuneration Policy.

6   You will be paid at monthly intervals on the last working day of the month in arrears to a bank account of your choice.

7   The Company leave year runs from the 1 April to 31 March. You are entitled to 28 leave days inclusive of public holidays.

8   You are obliged to give the Company four weeks' notice to terminate your contract of employment. The Company is obliged to give you the statutory minimum amount of notice before terminating your contract.

9   This post is subject to the completion of a three-month probationary period. At the end of this period, if your performance is of a satisfactory standard, your appointment will be made permanent. During this period, one week's notice may be given by either party to terminate this contract.

10   Your line manager must be notified as soon as practically possible in the case of sickness causing you to be unavailable for work, and appropriate certification must be provided.

11   In the course of your employment, you may have access to confidential information in both paper and electronic form. On no account should this be divulged to any unauthorised person. Breaches of confidentiality will be dealt with through the Company Policy and Procedure on Disciplinary Action.

12   You are referred to the Employee Handbook, the contents of which, taken together with these provisions, form part of your Contract of Employment.

Questions 21–27

Complete the notes below.

Choose **NO MORE THAN TWO WORDS AND/OR A NUMBER** from the text for each answer.

Terms and conditions of employment

- **Employer's name:** Mather Electronics Ltd

- **Job title: 21** .... *Marketing assistant*

- **Base:** Mather's **22** .... *Head Office*

- **Working hours:** 37.5 hours per week, including a daily
  23 .... *lunch break* *Lunch break*

- **Annual salary:** £22,500 plus **24** .... if any are given
  to team *bonuses*

- **Leave:** 28 days a year

- **Notice required to leave the company:** four weeks

- Appointment will be made permanent after a **25** .... *Probationary period*
  of three months

- Absence from work caused by **26** .... must be *sickness*
  reported at the earliest possible opportunity

- Disciplinary action may be taken if **27** .... is released
  × Breaches

Probationary period.
Breaches of Confidentially

Read the text below and answer Questions 28–40.

Wildlife in the South Atlantic

Lucy Grewcock on her trip to South Georgia

'Act like a penguin and you'll be accepted as a penguin,' Frank Todd, an expert in birds and our expedition leader, briefed us as we put on our life jackets and prepared to go ashore. Dropping anchor in South Georgia's Bay of Isles, we walked down the gangway into eight-person inflatable boats. Mine was the first to fill and we sped away with the engine revving loudly, leaving a swell of icy water in our wake.

Cold air filled our lungs as we raced towards the shore, which came alive with frantic fur seals splashing in the surf and wriggling up the beach beyond. It was like a holiday resort for the creatures and everyone in the boat was taking photographs.

Having embarked in Argentina, I'd spent over a week rocking and rolling across the Scotia Sea on board the M/S *Expedition* with 100 other passengers. And now, South Georgia seemed set to exceed expectations.

As we entered the shallows, the engine of the boat was cut and the air filled with the noises made by seal pups – a constant murmur beneath the barks and snorts of their parents, who moved awkwardly along the water's edge. Swinging our wellie-booted feet onto the beach, we pulled the inflatables ashore as a squad of seals shuffled over on their front flippers and cautioned us with sharp yellow teeth and low growls.

As I shook a trekking pole in defence, a party of well-dressed penguins paraded through a crowd of seal pups and waddled down the beach to welcome us, just as though they were human beings. One particularly smart adult stepped forward and casually waved a wing at the scene behind him. As I followed his gesture, I was astonished. While I knew we would see penguins, I had had no idea of the reality: they adorned the dunes in their thousands, packed out the plain beyond, and sprawled up the hillside until their silvery silhouettes merged into the horizon. We had arrived at one of the biggest penguin parties on the planet.

More than 100,000 of them populated the scene, and were bathed in a pool of golden light that radiated across them like a warm glow. But searching the sky for a break in the clouds, I saw nothing but a solid mass of grey mist over the bay. 'I think they look better in poor light,' Frank commented from behind me. 'They really shine, don't they?' I nodded in agreement, suddenly realising it was their yellow-tinged chins that were giving off the glow. Mesmerised, I picked my way across the pebble beach towards the colony, taking care not to squash the seal pups that fidgeted about my feet and doing my best to avoid their pugnacious parents.

Like a busy market, the penguin colony was in a constant state of murmur and mutter. Every few minutes, the hubbub was cut through by groups of adults, who would stretch their throats skywards, raise their beaks above the throng, and maintain contact with their chicks with a chorus of trumpet calls. Their calls were answered by the squeak of indignant chicks, who sat in thick fur coats, awaiting their next feed of fish. These infants take more than fourteen months to go from fur ball to fully watertight and, until then, are beach-bound and at the mercy of the petrels and skuas – predatory birds circling above and waiting for the opportunity to carry off a chick.

Distancing themselves from their squeaking siblings, adolescents waddled around in various stages of losing their juvenile feathers. In contrast, their parents stood in perfect penguin plumage, their coats acting as natural wetsuits, and each appeared to be wearing on its head a set of carrot-coloured earmuffs over a velvet-black hood – handsome markings which seemed to give them inner confidence.

Seeing the next lot of tourists arrive on the beach, I set off to find a quiet spot to take it all in. But as I clambered across the dunes, I had the feeling I was being followed and turned to find a penguin following me. Up to my waist in height, he wobbled along with his head down, his feet slipping across the stones. 'They are prone to being groupies,' Frank had warned us during our briefing. South Georgia's penguins have little reason to fear us. They have never been hunted by human beings, and their only visitors these days are groups of tourists and a scattering of scientists. Consequently, it appears, fear has been replaced with fascination.

Finding a patch of rough grass, I sat down and sighed contentedly. The beauty of this unspoilt wilderness was almost too much to take in. Gazing out across the bay at the immense glaciers and peaks beyond, I heard a shuffle of stones behind me and soon found my feathered follower standing by my shoulder. His eyes level with mine, the penguin followed my gaze out to sea, nodding his head as we took in the scene together. The pair of us stayed like that for a while, listening to the whimper of seal pups and watching the tide tickle the shoreline. 'Act like them, and you'll be accepted by them,' I smiled to myself. I'm sure he was thinking the same.

Questions 28–32

Complete the summary below.

*Choose **ONE WORD ONLY** from the text for each answer.*

Write your answers in boxes 28–32 on your answer sheet.

Landing in South Georgia

The expedition was led by Frank Todd, a specialist in the study of **28** ....
The journey began in **29** ...., and when the ship reached South Georgia, the
passengers transferred into small boats. As they approached the shore, they all wanted
30 .... of the seals on the beach. When the noise from the **31** ....
stopped, they could hear the young seals. As the group landed, some seals approached and
showed their **32** .... as a warning.

Questions 33–40

*Choose the correct letter, **A, B, C** or **D**.*

Write the correct letter in boxes 33–40 on your answer sheet.

33 According to the fifth paragraph, Lucy was surprised by

    A the lack of human beings.

    B the reaction of the seals.

    C the number of penguins.

    D the distance to the horizon.

34 What do Lucy and Frank agree about the penguins' appearance?

    A The dull light made part of them seem bright.

    B The sunshine made them shine.

    C Light was reflected onto them from the sea.

    D The mist made their white parts hard to see.

35 Lucy mentions a market to emphasise

    A the range of colours on the penguins and seals.

    B the noise made by the penguins.

    C the difference in behaviour between the penguins and the seals.

    D the contrast between the penguins' territory and surrounding areas.

36   Why did groups of adult penguins give 'trumpet calls'?

    A   to frighten the birds away

    B   to make sure they all kept close together

    C   to warn other penguins to keep away

    D   to communicate with their young

37   In the eighth paragraph, what does Lucy imagine about adult penguins?

    A   Those with damaged feathers stayed away from the others.

    B   They were more likely to move around than adolescents.

    C   They preferred to keep separate from adolescents.

    D   Their appearance influenced the way they felt.

38   Why did Lucy want to find a quiet spot?

    A   to look around her without being disturbed by other people

    B   to get away from the noise of the penguins and seals

    C   to look for a penguin that had become separated from the others

    D   to find somewhere suitable for the tourists to gather

39   What did Lucy learn in the briefing about the penguins of South Georgia?

    A   Their habitat has been damaged by the number of visitors.

    B   They are very interested in people.

    C   They are protected so that scientists can carry out research.

    D   They will not allow people to come close to them.

40   What did Lucy decide about the penguin that followed her?

    A   He had similar thoughts and feelings to her.

    B   He was more interested in the young seals than in her.

    C   He was a more suitable height for the terrain than her.

    D   He had more difficulty walking than she did.

WRITING TASK 1

You should spend about 20 minutes on this task.

> **You have recently travelled somewhere by train, but had several problems during the journey.**
>
> **Write a letter to the train company. In your letter**
>
> • **explain the reason for your journey**
> • **describe the problems you had on the journey**
> • **say what action you would like the train company to take.**

Write at least 150 words.

You do NOT need to write any addresses.

Begin your letter as follows:

Dear ...

WRITING TASK 2

You should spend about 40 minutes on this task.

Write about the following topic:

> **With developments in modern technology, it is much better to shop online.**
>
> **Do you agree or disagree?**

Give reasons for your answer and include any relevant examples from your own knowledge or experience.

Write at least 250 words.

General Training Test 2

SECTION 1   Questions 1–14

Read the text below and answer Questions 1–8.

Where to eat

in the city of **Bath** and the surrounding area

A Midtown Brasserie

Located in a former railway station, the Midtown Brasserie offers a relaxed, friendly environment with excellent, freshly prepared food and a jazz band playing every evening from Wednesday to Saturday. We have several 'celebrities' who use the restaurant regularly. This is a place for them to enjoy dining privately.

B The Bath Diner

Offering impressive views of the River Avon, The Bath Diner is well known for its Italian cuisine. A special menu is available for kids offering exciting pizzas and pasta. A much loved favourite in the historic city, it is close to the old Roman Baths.

C Green Park Hotel

The Head Chef designs the menus and will cater for any special meal requirements. He is always happy to create your favourite dishes. Set within award-winning gardens where the hotel grows organic vegetables and with gorgeous views over a beautiful valley, you can enjoy a traditional British afternoon tea on the terrace, or inside by the cosy fire.

D The Mary Jane

The Mary Jane is a luxurious floating restaurant and entertainment venue on the canal for private parties of 20–50 guests. We offer the perfect location for occasions like office parties, wedding receptions or conferences. There's also a range of special evenings available offering jazz in summer or you can organise your own musical entertainment.

E The Old Boat Restaurant

This family-run restaurant is 5–10 minutes' stroll from the city centre with beautiful views of the prettiest stretch of the River Avon. The restaurant serves British and European dishes. Rowing boats for hire from the boating station below help you to make a special day of it.

F The Black Horse

In a stunning hillside setting overlooking Bath spread out below, The Black Horse serves a wonderful menu of British flavours and produce. Surrounded by a spectacular landscape, the restaurant is just seven minutes' drive from central Bath.

G Riverside Café

Under Pulteney Bridge, on the banks of the River Avon, this restaurant has one of the best views in Bath. We always offer traditional dishes, fish, homemade meat or vegetable pies, and burgers and pasta. All the food is freshly prepared using fine local produce.

Questions 1–8

Look at the seven restaurant advertisements **A–G** on page 92.

For which restaurant are the following statements true?

*Write the correct letter, **A–G**, in boxes 1–8 on your answer sheet.*

NB *You may use any letter more than once.*

1   This restaurant has vegetarian dishes on its normal menu.

2   People can book this restaurant to celebrate a family event.

3   It is possible to hear live music here several days a week.

4   This restaurant is in a building that was originally used for a different purpose.

5   Guests can enjoy beautiful views of the whole city from this restaurant.

6   People who are allergic to certain foods can order specific dishes here.

7   This restaurant is on a boat.

8   At this restaurant guests can eat outside if they wish.

Learn kitesurfing with

The Kitesurf Centre at Camber Sands

Kitesurfing is a wind-powered watersport using a kite and a board. Although the word surfing is part of the name, suggesting a need for rough seas, calm water is perfect as it makes it easier to take off and land.

Being a new sport, kitesurfing takes its ideas from other sports, such as wakeboarding and powerkiting, and there is a lot of crossover. This allows you to pick up kitesurfing quickly and also improve on your other sport(s).

Kitesurfing has a lot of benefits healthwise as you use your whole body. Your legs are used to control the board and push against the power of the kite, while your upper body is used to hold onto the kite and keep your balance.

Even the largest kites pack up to fit in a rucksack and the boards are also relatively short, so there is no need to invest in a van to fit all your new kit in. The overall cost of the sport is relatively low as well, as once you've bought the kite and board, there's nothing left to pay for … the wind is free!

Each course has a maximum of four students per instructor and safety is the primary concern. The lesson durations are rough guides and the courses often overrun – we only finish when you've had a fun session and a good go at everything.

Our one-day kitesurfing course is aimed at complete beginners and is a great introduction to the sport. Initially, you learn the basics and kite control, while covering safety, location assessments, and kite set ups, then move into the water. The course is 90% practical and brilliant fun!

We also offer more advanced sessions. Have you ever found that you come back from a session having just cruised up and down without trying out anything new? With an experienced coach by your side to push you and aid your progress, you will improve much more!

Questions 9–14

Do the following statements agree with the information given in the text on page 94?

In boxes 9–14 on your answer sheet, write

TRUE   *if the statement agrees with the information*
FALSE   *if the statement contradicts the information*
NOT GIVEN   *if there is no information on this*

9   Large waves provide the best conditions for kitesurfing.

10   Kitesurfing has become more popular than wakeboarding and powerkiting.

11   Kitesurfing equipment is quite easy to transport.

12   The timing of kitesurfing lessons is very precise.

13   The one-day course includes how to choose good places to kitesurf.

14   Coaches encourage experienced kitesurfers to become more adventurous.

Read the text below and answer Questions 15–21.

JOB INTERVIEW TECHNIQUES
General hints and guidelines

Think about yourself

It is important before a job interview to think about why you are attending it and what you have to offer the organisation. Be ready to discuss both short and long term career goals in general terms.

You will also need to justify gaps in employment. If you worked in a temporary capacity but didn't put it on your CV, know the details of which companies you worked with, what you did for them and the length of the assignments. If you did not work but did search for a job, give some examples of the research you did regarding job opportunities and the process you went through to find a position.

Prepare to discuss your motivation for leaving your previous positions. If it was for a better opportunity, outline why it was better. If you were dismissed, present this in the most positive light you can.

Think about the organisation

Before attending any job interview, it is a good idea to research the organisation and have some well thought-out questions that would give you further information about it, for example, *How do you see the organisation developing over the next year / three years?*

What is the employer looking for?

Employers use interviews to confirm that applicants have the required knowledge, skills and willingness to become valued, trusted and productive team members.

You must try to consider how you can display your skills and experience in a good and honest light and provide employers with the evidence that you are the right person for the job, for example, whether you can work under pressure and manage your time effectively.

Recruiters look for an objective analysis of your abilities. For any strength, they want to know why you think it is one and where it has been demonstrated. For a weakness, they want to know what steps you could take to improve on it.

Points to consider throughout the interview

Prepare for the traditional cross-examination by rehearsing your answers, ideally with a friend who will give you honest feedback about the content and your body language. Concentrate on the employer's needs, not yours. Don't downplay your accomplishments or attribute them to luck. Finally, remember to request clarification if you are unsure of anything that is addressed to you.

Questions 15–21

Complete the sentences below.

*Choose **ONE WORD ONLY** from the text for each answer.*

Write your answers in boxes 15–21 on your answer sheet.

15   Be prepared to explain any .... you may have in your career record.

16   Be ready to talk about your .... for changing jobs in the past.

17   Find out about the company before the interview and prepare .... to increase your understanding of it.

18   Employers want to be given .... that a candidate is suitable for the post.

19   Any aspects of your character or working style that you have described as a .... will need to be justified.

20   Before the interview, practise what you intend to say and get .... from someone you can trust.

21   It is wise to ask for .... of any points that could be misunderstood.

Read the text below and answer Questions 22–27.

Start a business

How to start your own business

Running your own business is a rewarding but demanding career and life choice, but what is the best way to get started?

The first thing is the idea. This probably isn't a brand new invention or product. In fact, many successful small businesses have found a way to deliver an existing service or product more efficiently and economically or have customised an existing product or service to fit an opportunity.

Then you will need to put together a business plan. This doesn't require hundreds of pages with thousands of charts. Include research into things such as how much you can charge for your product/service, how much it will cost to produce or deliver (include variable and fixed costs) and the size of your potential market. The plan should evaluate your competitors – how many and how strong they are, where they are, how you will compete, etc. The plan should state what is required to enter this market, barriers to entry such as high fixed costs (factories, restaurants) and government regulations that must be met.

Your business plan should include a section on how you intend to finance your start-up. How will you pay the costs to start and run your business? Do you need a bank loan? Will you use credit cards? Also, you'll need to consider how much salary you need to support yourself while starting your business.

You will also need an initial marketing plan. Marketing need not cost a fortune. Some businesses require very little. For example, many service businesses such as accounting firms build their practices through existing customers' referrals when they are satisfied with the service they receive. You can also join low-cost local associations to build awareness of your small business. Again, your business plan (product, customer, competitor) will help you determine the marketing efforts you need to undertake.

Build your infrastructure early. This doesn't mean build a big factory or a fancy office. It simply means keep accurate records. One of the downfalls of many small businesses is that they don't know if they're making or losing money. Another downfall is when small business owners try to sell their company years later but lack accurate customer history and customer information. Many times, the customers of a small business are its best asset.

Now you can move forward. Once you know you can be profitable, take the leap and get started.

Questions 22–27

Complete the notes below.

Choose **ONE WORD ONLY** from the text for each answer.

Write your answers in boxes 22–27 on your answer sheet.

Starting your own business

- **Idea:** probably based on an existing product/service

- **Business plan:** should include

    - costs of production/delivery

    - number of possible customers

    - assessment of **22** .... already operating in the field

    - details of state **23** .... to be observed

    - consideration of the way you will **24** .... the setting up of your business

    - decision on size of personal salary required

- **Marketing:** can be achieved

    - free through **25** .... from customers

    - cheaply by becoming a member of **26** .... in the area

- **Infrastructure:** depends mainly on maintaining clear **27** .... from the start

State (verb?)

Questions 28–33

The text on page 101 and 102 has six paragraphs, **A–F**.

Choose the correct heading for each paragraph from the list of headings below.

Write the correct number, **i–ix**, in boxes 28–33 on your answer sheet.

List of Headings

   i   Birds whose behaviour is unique

  ii   Why cranes are valued in the culture of Bhutan

 iii   An increase in international tourism

  iv   What makes the wetlands attractive to cranes

   v   A policy of protecting the cranes by attracting visitors

  vi   The problems that success might cause

 vii   How cranes typically behave in the course of a year

viii   The effects of climate change on the cranes' habitat

  ix   Undesirable consequences of social changes

---

28 Paragraph **A**

29 Paragraph **B**

30 Paragraph **C**

31 Paragraph **D**

32 Paragraph **E**

33 Paragraph **F**

Festival of *flight*

Each year, thousands of people gather in the South Asian kingdom of Bhutan's remote Phobjikha Valley for the Black-Necked Crane Festival, a contribution to the conservation of this endangered species.

Julia Horton reports.

A   Black-necked cranes were the last of the world's fifteen crane species to be discovered, found in the Himalayas on the remote Tibetan plateau in 1876 by the Russian naturalist Count Nikolai Przhevalsky. They are renowned for their 'dancing' behaviours, which include bowing, jumping and wing flapping. These activities are associated with courtship and are also believed to strengthen the pair bonds that form between male and female birds. The cranes, which reach a height of about 140 centimetres and have a 235-centimetre wingspan, are confined to the plateau and neighbouring regions, breeding in high mountain wetlands during spring and summer before migrating to lower altitudes for the winter. For centuries, their arrival in Bhutan – which usually begins in late October – has marked the end of the harvest season and signalled time for farmers and their families to move to lower, warmer altitudes.

B   But changes in traditional farming practices throughout the birds' range are threatening to destroy their habitat. These risks have resulted in them being placed on the IUCN's (International Union for Conservation of Nature) Red List of Threatened Species; they are currently categorised as 'vulnerable'. Censuses carried out throughout the birds' range suggest that the total population could be as high as 11,000 or as low as 8,800. About 500 cranes winter in Bhutan each year, mostly in Phobjikha, the kingdom's largest wetland and most important black-necked crane habitat. They come to feed on the remains of the autumn harvest in the local agricultural fields, as well as on bamboos that grow in the valley's wetlands, which they supplement with seeds, earthworms, beetles and snails. In recognition of Phobjikha's importance to the birds, a conservation area was established in the valley in 2003.

C   The conservation festival which takes place when the cranes return to Bhutan from Tibet for the winter, was started recently by the Royal Society for the Protection of Nature (RSPN). Its aim is to promote ecotourism to provide the valley's farmers with an alternative income, in order to reduce the pressure on the birds' habitat. To this end, the 150 villagers who dance in the festival are paid 150 Ngultrums (£2) each for their performance. It may not sound like much, but with almost a quarter of the country living below the poverty line, it is welcome nonetheless. Recently, a group of entrepreneurial farmers have also begun offering homestays. As one of the main organisers of the event, Dawazam is among the most enlightened of the villagers, who now run the festival themselves. 'Thanks to the festival, everyone here is very well informed [about the fact] that if they don't harm the cranes, we will have lots of people coming here,' she says.

D   While livelihoods are important, the festival is also aimed at strengthening traditional celebrations to help increase villagers' awareness of the birds' importance – and the threats to their existence. Known as 'thrung thrung karm' in the local language, the cranes symbolise long life to the Bhutanese and are considered to be holy. People believe that the circling of the cranes as they come in to land confers a special blessing, so the winter wheat is not sown until after this has been received.

E   'Local people have a respect for the black-necked crane that is related to their culture,' says Tshering Choki of the RSPN. 'People would never eat these birds, but what they don't understand is that they can damage their habitat indirectly. There are more and more settlements with people wanting more agriculture. Our main concern is about the use of agrochemicals [such as chemical fertilisers]. If we're not careful and don't educate people, there is a chance that they could have an impact on the birds' feeding area.' In the past, Choki explains, neighbours would help to work each others' land, but now, they often have to pay people to be labourers. Simply using agrochemicals to improve yields is easier and cheaper. Changing land use has also threatened the cranes' wintering grounds. About 30 years ago, the government of Bhutan began distributing public land in the valley near the birds' habitat to landless locals so that they could start growing potatoes to supplement the traditional wheat crop. There was also talk of draining the wetlands and turning them over to potatoes. Soon after, the process was stopped when the RSPN intervened, pointing out the importance of the land for crane conservation. By then, however, large areas of ground had already become private property.

F   Ironically, while the festival organisers would like to attract some foreign visitors to support conservation, there are fears that tourism businesses keen for a share of the action will destroy the very thing that draws people here. Choki says, 'We're worried because there are some people from outside this area of Bhutan who want to invest in tourism here, by building lodges, for example. That will also increase the population even more, bringing more people from other parts of Bhutan looking for jobs in the lodges.' This will in turn lead to more land being used to build accommodation.

Questions 34–36

Complete the summary below.

*Choose **ONE WORD ONLY** from the text for each answer.*

Write your answers in boxes 34–36 on your answer sheet.

BLACK-NECKED CRANES

People admire this species of crane for the different forms of dancing they exhibit. These are thought to form part of the birds' **34** .... habits. The cranes breed high up in the Himalayas and then migrate to Bhutan. By the time they arrive, the farmers are finishing the **35** .... The cranes then spend the winter in wetland areas, such as Phobjikha valley, where they survive mainly on plants, like the **36** .... that grow there.

Questions 37–40

*Choose the correct letter, **A**, **B**, **C** or **D**.*

Write the correct letter in boxes 37–40 on your answer sheet.

37 Why was the festival started?

    A   to raise awareness of traditional farming

    B   to try to maintain the cranes' winter habitat

    C   to increase local people's income by organising homestays

    D   to develop a tourist destination in Bhutan for the autumn season

38 The people of Bhutan consider the cranes to be particularly important because

    A   their arrival coincides with the right weather to sow wheat.

    B   they see them as sacred creatures which benefit both people and crops.

    C   their return marks an opportunity to have local gatherings.

    D   they are thought to be unusually long lived as a species.

39 Choki believes that education is necessary to make people understand

    A   which type of crops to grow in the valley.

    B   what the best way is to help their neighbours.

    C   what chemical fertilisers could do to the land.

    D   how many farms there should be in each settlement.

40 What concerns the RSPN at the moment?

    A   Tourists will soon forget about the cranes.

    B   The number of unemployed will increase considerably.

    C   Foreign companies will take over the running of the festival.

    D   Their original aim in starting the festival will not be achieved.

WRITING

WRITING TASK 1

You should spend about 20 minutes on this task.

> ***You have just completed an evening course at your local college.***
>
> ***Write a letter to the college. In your letter:***
>
> - ***describe the course you took***
> - ***explain what you liked and disliked about it***
> - ***suggest how it could be improved.***

Write at least 150 words.

You do NOT need to write any addresses.

Begin your letter as follows:

Dear ...

WRITING TASK 2

You should spend about 40 minutes on this task.

Write about the following topic:

> *More and more people are travelling by car nowadays.*
>
> *What are the reasons for the increase in car use and what problems does it cause?*
>
> *What can be done to discourage people from using their cars?*

Give reasons for your answer and include any relevant examples from your own knowledge or experience.

Write at least 250 words.

Answer key

Test 1

LISTENING

SECTION 1

1	Monday	**6**	buildings
2	23rd	**7**	style
3	215	**8**	street
4	Crabtree	**9**	gallery
5	digital	**10**	discount

SECTION 2

11 B
12 C
13 B
14 A
15 A
16 C
17 and **18** A and D *[in either order]*
19 and **20** A and B *[in either order]*

SECTION 3

21	C/E	**26**	nursery (staff)
22	E/C	**27**	material(s)
23	B/D	**28**	cardboard
24	D/B	**29**	script
25	(birthday) party	**30**	colourful / colorful

SECTION 4

31	neighbour	**36**	assumptions
32	frustration	**37**	extrovert / extravert
33	relationships	**38**	arrogant
34	gestures	**39**	professor
35	gender	**40**	goals

ACADEMIC READING

PASSAGE 1

1	counter	**7**	(the) population
2	residents	**8**	FALSE
3	coins	**9**	TRUE
4	travellers	**10**	NOT GIVEN
5	(an / the) ordinary / ordinaries	**11**	FALSE
		12	TRUE
6	(cheap) snacks	**13**	NOT GIVEN

PASSAGE 2

14	D	**21**	D
15	H	**22**	A
16	F	**23**	Great Exhibition
17	B	**24**	flexible
18	D	**25**	terminus
19	C	**26**	iron, glass *[in either order]*
20	A		

PASSAGE 3

27	C	**34**	NOT GIVEN
28	B	**35**	YES
29	D	**36**	NO
30	A	**37**	B
31	D	**38**	E
32	YES	**39**	A
33	NOT GIVEN	**40**	C

ACADEMIC WRITING   MODEL ANSWERS

TASK 1

The charts give information on temperature and rainfall in two Australian cities – Sydney and Darwin – by month. Clearly Darwin is consistently hotter than Sydney, while Sydney experiences less rainfall overall.

Darwin's average maximum temperature hardly changes throughout the year, only varying within the very narrow range of 30 to 33 degrees. In contrast, the corresponding figures for Sydney vary much more, with a high of 26 degrees in December, January and February, and a dip to 16 degrees in July.

The two cities also differ considerably as regards rainfall, though in this case Darwin sees much greater variation during the year. Here, rainfall is mainly concentrated between December and March, with a high of about 425 mm in January. May to September is extremely dry, with virtually no rain at all from June to August.

In Sydney, on the other hand, there is much less variation in monthly totals. There is less rain than in Darwin from November to March, and more in the rest of the year. The highest figure is in June, with about 130 mm, and the lowest is about 70 mm in October.

TASK 2

When I was a child, most people seemed to have plenty of spare time to go for walks, sit and read, or do other things that they regarded as enjoyable, but not essential. Nowadays, however, if I suggest to a friend that we go out for a meal or go to the cinema, the chances are they'll reply that they would love to, but they're too busy.

One cause of this change is that work patterns are different. In many companies and public sector organisations, work is now highly pressured: people often have to stay in the office late, or catch up with work when they get home. Despite the drawbacks of this sort of working life, it is rare for people to give it up, because to do so would seriously affect their standard of living.

Another cause is that many young people spend significant amounts of time studying for exams and qualifications in order to improve their chances in the very competitive job market. This can leave them with very little time to do other things, such as sport or visiting friends and relatives.

It is hard to see how this situation could be changed, as I think it requires a major shift in public values: we need to spend less money, work less and relax more, but until most people recognise and accept that, the change is unlikely to take place. Perhaps all that can be done is to take every opportunity to talk about the benefits of free time and the dangers of working long hours.

I think it is unlikely that this situation will improve. If anything, it may well get worse.

SPEAKING — MODEL ANSWERS

PART 1

Examiner	Good morning/afternoon.
Candidate	Good morning/afternoon.
Examiner	Can you tell me your full name, please?
Candidate	Monika Bauer.
Examiner	And what shall I call you?
Candidate	Mo, please.
Examiner	And can you tell me where you're from?
Candidate	I'm originally from Germany.
Examiner	Can I see your identification, please?
Candidate	Here you are. [Show your ID]

Examiner	Let's talk about your home country. Which country do you live in now?
Candidate	I live in France.
Examiner	How much of your life have you lived there?
Candidate	I've lived there since I moved from Germany, five years ago.
Examiner	How would you describe the people from your country?
Candidate	People from Germany are very clever. They are often interested in green issues. Some people say they don't have a sense of humour, but this is not true. They like music and they like having a good time.
Examiner	Which area in your country do you like most?
Candidate	I like Bavaria because it is very beautiful. I used to go on holiday there and I loved those holidays. It is very different from other parts of Germany. It is very traditional and the buildings and the countryside are very interesting.
Examiner	Let's move on to talk about ...

PART 2

Examiner	Can you start speaking now, please?
Candidate	The person who helped me was my friend, Sarah. She helped me when I had to move about three years ago. I was renting a flat, and then the landlord told me I had to move out. So I had to quickly find a new place. I was lucky, because I found a small house in the same area. But I had to move quickly, and Sarah was brilliant. She helped me pack all my things into boxes, and took stuff to the new place in her car on the day I moved. Then she helped me clean the old place and the new place. She even cooked some meals for me while I was busy sorting everything out. I couldn't have done it all without her.
Examiner	Do you like this person?
Candidate	Yes, of course!
Examiner	Do you think helping other people is important?
Candidate	Very.

PART 3

Examiner	We've been talking about a time when a person helped you and I'd like to discuss with you one or two more general questions related to this. Let's consider first of all helping people at home. What help can people who live together give each other every day?
Candidate	They can help each other by cleaning, cooking, that kind of thing. And listening to their problems, trying to help.
Examiner	What are the advantages of asking for help from family members rather than friends?
Candidate	Family members probably know you better, so they can make more useful suggestions. Because they're your family, they're more likely to want to help you. It's a reciprocal thing, too – they help you and you help them when they need help.
Examiner	Whose responsibility is it to care for the rising number of old people in most societies?
Candidate	It's nicer for old people to be looked after by their families, but not everyone has family members that can do this. So the government has to do it. Because people work in their societies and pay their taxes, they should be able to expect a good quality of care when they are too old to look after themselves. It's a sign of a civilised society.
Examiner	Thank you. That is the end of the Speaking test.

Test 2

LISTENING

SECTION 1

1 MACARTHUR
2 (reading) glasses
3 215
4 brown
5 14(th) Feb(ruary) / 14/2 / 2/14
6 (the / train / railway) station
7 brother
8 black hair
9 wallet
10 student property

SECTION 2

11	127	16	I
12	holiday village	17	E
13	Aim High	18	C
14	local industry	19	D
15	sunset	20	F

SECTION 3

21	A	26	D
22	B	27	B
23	C	28	F
24	C	29	A
25	A	30	B

SECTION 4

31	feathers	36	collision
32	(black) cloud	37	magnified
33	mid-winter	38	critical list
34	feeding places	39	literature
35	cameras	40	Central Park

ACADEMIC READING

PASSAGE 1

1	FALSE	8	FALSE
2	TRUE	9	NOT GIVEN
3	NOT GIVEN	10	(a) painting
4	FALSE	11	rocks
5	TRUE	12	(a) poem
6	FALSE	13	(a) pond / water
7	NOT GIVEN		

PASSAGE 2

14 C
15 F
16 B
17 A
18 C
19 and 20 C and D [in either order]
21 dullness
22 frequently / often
23 year
24 paradox
25 president
26 non(-)existence

PASSAGE 3

27	D	34	NOT GIVEN
28	A	35	YES
29	C	36	NO
30	B	37	rhubarb
31	C	38	symptoms
32	A	39	expensive
33	YES	40	advantage

TASK 1

The charts provide information on the transportation of goods from the eastern and western regions of a country.

One significant difference is in the use of road transport, although it is the largest category in both areas of the country. In the eastern region this accounts for 60 per cent of goods moved, well over half the total, while the figure drops to 35 per cent for the western region.

Rail transport is the second largest category for both regions, at 20 per cent in the east, and 25 per cent in the western region. However, river and canal is the means of transporting only 10 per cent of goods in both regions.

In the east, pipeline and air transport are both at low levels, accounting for only 5 per cent each of total goods transported. However, a very different picture appears in the western region, with pipeline transport at 20 per cent, and air at 10.

Overall, there is a more even spread of modes of transport in the western region than in the east, where road transport is the largest category by far.

TASK 2

In my country, almost everyone lived in a family unit until about thirty years ago, but now it is increasingly common for people to live alone and this is having a significant impact on society.

There are several reasons for the change. One is that improvements in healthcare mean that, on average, people live much longer than in the past. As a result, if a husband or wife dies, their spouse may well stay alive for many years, possibly living alone. Another factor is that couples are far more likely to get divorced now than in the past, which means that one of them will probably move out of the family home and live on his or her own.

In addition, social attitudes are changing. In the past, people who lived alone were often pitied, or regarded as eccentric, because it was generally assumed that nobody would choose to live in that way. Nowadays, it is far more acceptable, and the people concerned may even be envied.

In my opinion, the impact of this trend on the individual is positive as it means there is a greater choice of lifestyle. People who would be happier living alone, or who are difficult to live with, are no longer under social pressure to live in a family. Being able to choose one's own way of living must make for greater happiness. On the other hand, society as a whole can suffer from the trend. The more single-person households there are, the more small homes are required. However, many countries have too little accommodation of a suitable size, and too many larger houses with only one resident.

On balance, I think the increase in single-person households is a positive development, but more should be done to match housing to changing requirements.

SPEAKING   MODEL ANSWERS

PART 1

Examiner	Good morning/afternoon.
Candidate	Good morning/afternoon.
Examiner	Can you tell me your full name, please?
Candidate	Carlos Benitez.
Examiner	And what shall I call you?
Candidate	Carlos.
Examiner	And can you tell me where you're from?
Candidate	I'm from Madrid, Spain.
Examiner	Can I see your identification, please?
Candidate	Here you are. *[Show your ID]*

Examiner	Let's talk about what you do. Do you work or are you a student?
Candidate	I work.
Examiner	What job do you do?
Candidate	I'm an accountant.
Examiner	How did you find this job?
Candidate	I saw it in an advertisement in a newspaper. I applied and had an interview.
Examiner	How long do you think you will continue doing this job?
Candidate	I hope I'll do it until I retire.
Examiner	Can you describe a typical day for you at work?
Candidate	I get to work at 8.30. I turn on the computer. I answer some emails and then if I haven't got any meetings, I write some reports. I have lunch at about 12.30 and in the afternoon I often go and visit some suppliers. I leave work at about 5.30.
Examiner	Let's move on to talk about ...

PART 2

Examiner	Can you start speaking now, please?
Candidate	One meal I enjoyed a lot was the meal I had to celebrate my eighteenth birthday. I went with all of my family to a restaurant in the countryside. It used to be a flour mill, but now it's the best restaurant in our area, in my opinion. There were 30 of us at the meal: my parents, my sister and my brother, my aunts, uncles and cousins, and we all sat around one very long table. It was quite a hot day in spring, and we sat outside under some grape vines. We ate all kinds of meat and vegetable dishes, and some salads. I've forgotten some of the dishes, but I do remember eating some delicious squid, though, and I remember that I ate everything very happily! I enjoyed it such a lot because I was with my family and we all get on very well. I was very happy to be eighteen, and I was given lots of fantastic presents by my family and friends.

Examiner	Would you like to have the same meal again?
Candidate	Yes, I would.
Examiner	Do you like cooking meals for other people?
Candidate	Not much!

PART 3

Examiner	We've been talking about eating and food and I'd like to discuss with you one or two more general questions related to this. At which special times do families or friends eat a meal together in your country?
Candidate	Families in my country usually eat together on special holiday days, like at Christmas and Easter, and on some saints' days.
Examiner	Do you agree or disagree that families should eat at least one meal together every day?
Candidate	I agree that families should eat together at least once a day. I think family relationships are very important, but you have to work hard to keep those relationships strong. You need to meet and talk to each other to find out what's going on with the members of your family, and then you can all support each other.
Examiner	Explain how some kinds of food can damage your health.
Candidate	Most of the problems with food are related to having too much food of one kind or another. If you have just a little of any kind of food, it is unlikely to do you very much harm. However, if you have too much sweet food or fatty food, this can have serious effects on your health. But even if you have too much of some kinds of healthy food, this is bad for you, too. For example, eating too many carrots can make you ill.
Examiner	Thank you. That is the end of the Speaking test.

Test 3

LISTENING

SECTION 1

1	competitions	**6**	monthly
2	refreshments	**7**	mountains
3	repair kit	**8**	charity
4	DOUGLEY	**9**	221337
5	knees	**10**	get outside / getoutside

SECTION 2

11	lost art	**16**	quiet
12	drawings	**17**	paper
13	secrets	**18**	tool
14	shoe(-)box	**19**	question
15	diary	**20**	ending

SECTION 3

21 and **22** A and D *[in either order]*
23 and **24** B and E *[in either order]*
25 A
26 B
27 B
28 C
29 A
30 C

SECTION 4

31 patience
32 relevance
33 recipe
34 memorisation / memorization
35 principles
36 budget
37 literacy
38 statistics
39 foundation
40 measurement

ACADEMIC READING

PASSAGE 1

1	TRUE	**8**	liquid
2	NOT GIVEN	**9**	broken
3	FALSE	**10**	terracotta / clay
4	TRUE	**11**	gold
5	carved	**12**	learning
6	clay	**13**	conquest
7	melts		

PASSAGE 2

14 iv
15 iii
16 vi
17 viii
18 v
19 vii
20 i
21 and **22** A and D *[in either order]*
23 C
24 B
25 A
26 C

PASSAGE 3

27	B	**34**	YES
28	D	**35**	NOT GIVEN
29	A	**36**	NOT GIVEN
30	D	**37**	YES
31	C	**38**	E
32	NO	**39**	B
33	NO	**40**	A

ACADEMIC WRITING   MODEL ANSWERS

TASK 1

The diagram illustrates the process for making bricks. This is a fairly straightforward process that involves a number of stages and some basic equipment.

First, a digger is used to dig clay out of the ground. This is passed through a metal grid and over a roller to break it into small pieces. Sand and water are then added, and after this the mixture is ready to be turned into bricks. It can be poured into individual brick moulds, or passed through an extruder unit and then cut into bricks with a wire cutter. Whichever way the bricks are formed, they are subsequently placed in a drying oven for one or two days. Next they are placed in a moderate kiln, at temperatures between 200 °C and 980 °C, followed by a high-temperature kiln, which is at temperatures of 870 to 1,300 °C. Finally, the bricks are left in a cooling chamber for 48 to 72 hours.

Once the bricks are finished and ready for use, they are packaged and loaded onto a lorry for delivery to the customer or retail outlet.

TASK 2

Advertising has a long history, but consumerism has made it a major part of our lives. This is a consequence of the enormous number of companies competing with each other and the numerous methods of advertising that are now available. In a single day we are likely to see advertisements in newspapers, on television, at the cinema, online, in the street and on our mobile phones. In order to attract our attention, advertising is constantly becoming more sophisticated and more intrusive.

From the point of view of the general public, there is too much advertising. It is likely to be of little or no interest in itself, except when it relates to items we intend to buy, or is entertaining or interesting. The majority of adverts force themselves on our attention, distracting us from what we're trying to do and leaving us with a sense of being harrassed.

However, for the organisations trying to sell their products or services, advertising is essential: without it, they will soon go out of business. They not only need to make their adverts more memorable than those of their competitors – and give consumers positive feelings towards the product – they also have to keep reminding us about the product. So from their point of view, there is not too much advertising.

Given the level of consumerism and competition in modern societies, the amount of advertising we have is unavoidable. Ideally, governments should take steps to limit any increase, for instance, by banning adverts on private land adjoining roads and by restricting the amount of television time that can be devoted to commercials. For me, at least, there is far too much advertising.

PART 1

Examiner	Good morning/afternoon.
Candidate	Good morning/afternoon.
Examiner	Can you tell me your full name, please?
Candidate	Philippe Germont.
Examiner	And what shall I call you?
Candidate	Please call me Philippe.
Examiner	And can you tell me where you're from?
Candidate	I'm from a small village in eastern France.
Examiner	Can I see your identification, please?
Candidate	Here you are. *[Show your ID]*

Examiner	Let's talk about what you do. Do you work or are you a student?
Candidate	I'm a student.
Examiner	What subject or subjects do you study?
Candidate	Maths.
Examiner	How long have you been studying this subject?
Candidate	Since I started school when I was five.
Examiner	What do you enjoy most about studying this subject?
Candidate	I enjoy finding the answers to maths problems. When I've spent a long time trying to find an answer, it's very satisfying to finally work out the answer. It's good when no one else has succeeded too!
Examiner	What other subject would you like to study?
Candidate	I'd like to study art because it is very different to maths and that would give me balance. I'd like to go to art galleries and know about the artists and then learn to paint and draw for myself.
Examiner	Let's move on to talk about …

PART 2

Examiner	Can you start speaking now, please?
Candidate	When I was a student, I used to cycle everywhere. I had an old bike which my dad bought for me. I cycled everywhere because public transport wasn't very good where I lived and I couldn't afford a car. Most of my friends cycled, too. I used to enjoy cycling in the summer, when the weather was good, but in the winter, cycling was usually awful. The worst thing was windy weather, because it made it really difficult to cycle. But thanks to the cycling, I felt really fit.
Examiner	Would you recommend this activity to other people?
Candidate	Yes, I would.
Examiner	Did you find the activity easy?
Candidate	Not really.

PART 3

Examiner	We've been talking about an activity you've done to help you stay healthy and I'd like to discuss with you one or two more general questions related to this. Let's consider first of all staying healthy. What activities make people unhealthy?
Candidate	Activities which do not require a lot of activity can make you unhealthy. For example, if you spend a lot of time sitting on the sofa watching TV or playing computer games, you increase your chances of becoming unhealthy.
Examiner	Do you agree or disagree that young children have healthier lifestyles than teenagers?
Candidate	I agree that young children's lifestyles are healthier. This is because they are generally more active than teenagers. They like playing outside, and running around with their friends during break times at school, for example. Their parents can also control what they eat, too, so they usually have a healthier diet.
Examiner	How much do you think people's jobs affect how healthy they are?
Candidate	I think your work can affect your health a lot. For example, a coal miner can get very ill from work-related illnesses that affect breathing. Before smoking was banned, waiting staff in restaurants and pubs could get heart and lung diseases from their work environment. On the other hand, your work can help you stay healthy. If you are a postal worker, for instance, who walks to deliver the mail, then you might be quite fit.
Examiner	Thank you. That is the end of the Speaking test.

Test 4

LISTENING

SECTION 1

1 Saturday
2 11.30 (p.m.)
3 (music / musical) concert
4 disabled
5 sandwiches
6 piano
7 coach
8 225
9 JEZOWSKI
10 07232855496

SECTION 2

11 F
12 G
13 A
14 C
15 B
16 H
17 and 18 C and D *[in either order]*
19 and 20 B and C *[in either order]*

SECTION 3

21 C
22 A
23 A
24 C
25 B
26 A
27 and 28 B and D *[in either order]*
29 and 30 B and C *[in either order]*

SECTION 4

31 C
32 A
33 B
34 bucket
35 lines
36 smell
37 (a) weight
38 (a / the) railway / (the) railways
39 1847
40 Observatory / observatory

ACADEMIC READING

PASSAGE 1

1 NOT GIVEN
2 FALSE
3 TRUE
4 FALSE
5 NOT GIVEN
6 TRUE
7 marble
8 ramp
9 mirror
10 ropes
11 food
12 earthquake
13 fortress

PASSAGE 2

14 F
15 D
16 A
17 E
18 B
19 turmeric
20 buffalo(s)
21 scientists
22 summer
23 and 24 A and C *[in either order]*
25 and 26 B and E *[in either order]*

PASSAGE 3

27 B
28 A
29 A
30 D
31 C
32 H
33 F
34 E
35 YES
36 NOT GIVEN
37 NO
38 NOT GIVEN
39 YES
40 NO

TASK 1

The bar chart provides information on the value of sales for four different types of products at a particular store, in the three years 2010 to 2012.

The highest value category in all three years was soaps and handwash, which started the period with sales worth $150,000, saw a large rise to $180,000 in 2011, and another increase, although a smaller one to $187,000 in 2012.

In 2010, the sales value of the other three categories were roughly equal, at around $70,000. However, over the three-year period, that of shower gels increased considerably, reaching $120,000 in 2012. The value of shampoo sales experienced a slight increase in 2011, but sales fell to $60,000 in 2012. Meanwhile, the sales value of hair conditioners dipped to $60,000 in 2011, but recovered in 2012, ending the period a little higher than at the beginning, at nearly $80,000.

Overall, sales values increased for three of the product categories between 2010 and 2012, but decreased for shampoos. This was the only category where sales were worth less than at the beginning.

TASK 2

People who are unfit are limited in their work and leisure choices, and run a greater risk of contracting various illnesses. Their lack of fitness can also have a negative impact on society as a whole, so it is important to encourage people to do some exercise.

An unfit individual may find it difficult to do a job that involves moving quickly, and even going for a stroll in the countryside can be a problem. Perhaps family members need to look after them, and that restricts what those relations have time to do. If the individual falls ill, colleagues may need to do some of their work.

Society at large is also affected. Expenditure on healthcare, by governments and individuals, is enormous. If people did more exercise, the cost would be reduced, which in turn could mean lower taxes.

Although there is little doubt of the benefits of regular exercise, it can be time-consuming and unrewarding, so people are unlikely to do much exercise unless they really want to. They need encouragement.

In my opinion, the easiest way to exercise is to do it in a way that disguises the fact. Playing football, or walking to work or school, is a good incentive because it is an end in itself, with improved fitness as a side-effect, whereas going to a gym is purely to do exercise.

It would be useful if health organisations ran advertising campaigns suggesting ways of improving fitness that aren't limited to the gym and jogging; some governments already encourage people to walk rather than drive short distances, or point out the health benefits of using a bicycle.

Improving a nation's fitness is an uphill struggle, and progress will inevitably be very slow. However, even very gradual improvements would eventually benefit both the individual concerned and other people.

SPEAKING MODEL ANSWERS

PART 1

Examiner	Good morning/afternoon.
Candidate	Good morning/afternoon.
Examiner	Can you tell me your full name, please?
Candidate	Susanne Gerbner.
Examiner	And what shall I call you?
Candidate	Suzi, please.
Examiner	And can you tell me where you're from?
Candidate	I'm from a small town near Zurich, in Switzerland.
Examiner	Can I see your identification, please?
Candidate	Here you are. *[Show your ID]*
Examiner	Let's talk about public transport. Do you like using public transport, for example, buses and trains?
Candidate	Yes, because it's cheap and I don't like driving.
Examiner	What kinds of public transport are available in your town?
Candidate	There are buses, trams and trains.
Examiner	Which would you choose if you were going on a long journey: a bus or a train?
Candidate	I'd go on a train because it's much faster and you can walk about on a train. It's more comfortable than a bus and they have a shop where you can buy snacks and drinks.
Examiner	How would you improve public transport in your town?
Candidate	I would change the route of the tram. I'd make it longer. At the moment, it only stops at a few places and it doesn't go near my flat. It's also quite expensive, so I would make it cheaper.
Examiner	Let's move on to talk about …

PART 2

Examiner	Can you start speaking now, please?
Candidate	Last year, I went to a street festival that made me feel very happy. It was in the summer, and everyone who went was really happy. There were thousands of people there, but there was no trouble. In fact, the police joined in with the dancing! The festival was called the Free Street Festival. It was a long parade of about 50 floats, with dancers, clowns, acrobats and musicians. The atmosphere was fantastic. I danced all day, but didn't feel tired at all. It was just a really joyful day for everyone.
Examiner	Would you like this event to happen again?
Candidate	Yes!
Examiner	Do you have any souvenirs of that event?
Candidate	Yes, a T-shirt.

PART 3

Examiner	We've been talking about an event that made you feel happy. I'd like to discuss with you one or two more general questions related to this. Let's consider first of all having a good time. What kind of activities do most people do to have a good time?
Candidate	People go out. They go and see a film, or go dancing at a club, or they go out with friends for dinner, or to the pub.
Examiner	How does the way we have a good time change as we get older?
Candidate	As we get older, we like doing different things. For example, when we're young and single, we go out dancing or doing sports which we find more difficult when we're older. Also, when we're older, we might get married and have children, so we can't go out so easily, and we enjoy spending time at home with our family.
Examiner	Would you like to spend your whole life just having a good time?
Candidate	I don't know. It might be a bit boring! I think you'd run out of entertaining things to do, and you might not enjoy them so much anyway. Sometimes, it's really nice to do very simple things, like having a long breakfast for example, just because if you work, you don't usually have time to.
Examiner	Thank you. That is the end of the Speaking test.

General Training Test 1

READING

SECTION 1

1 D
2 B
3 A
4 B
5 E
6 C
7 A
8 D
9 TRUE
10 TRUE
11 FALSE
12 NOT GIVEN
13 NOT GIVEN
14 FALSE

SECTION 2

15 merger
16 turnover
17 consultation
18 survey
19 induction
20 external
21 marketing assistant
22 Head Office
23 lunch break
24 bonus(es)
25 probationary period
26 sickness
27 confidential information

SECTION 3

28 birds
29 Argentina
30 photo(graphs)
31 engine / boat
32 teeth
33 C
34 A
35 B
36 D
37 D
38 A
39 B
40 A

WRITING MODEL ANSWERS

TASK 1

Dear Sir,

I am writing to complain about some problems that I had recently while travelling by train.

Last Tuesday I caught the 8.30 a.m. train from Exeter to London. I had a meeting which started at 11 a.m. and it was very important that I got there on time. The train left according to schedule, but half an hour into the journey, it suddenly stopped. The train driver told us that there was a problem with the engine and that an engineer was on his way. He assured us that he would be there in ten minutes. We waited for one hour and nothing happened. Finally we started moving, but just to the next station, where we all had to get out and wait for another train. It was freezing cold on the platform and the waiting room was not open. Another train finally arrived, but by then it was 12.00, which was much too late for my meeting in London.

I have enclosed my ticket and would like you to refund the money as soon as possible. I look forward to hearing from you.

Yours faithfully,

TASK 2

These days, more and more people are shopping online. This certainly has a number of advantages. Firstly, it can be very convenient and save a lot of time. When people are working long hours, they may not have time to go shopping, or the shops may be closed when they finish work. Another advantage is that if you go online you can look at different websites and compare prices more easily. By doing this, you can make sure you get the best deal and save a lot of money. It is also very important to consider the enormous benefits online shopping has brought to those people who are old or disabled and cannot leave their homes easily or carry shopping home.

However, there are also many drawbacks to online shopping. One of the obvious ones is that it is more difficult to judge a product if you can only see it on screen. This is particularly important when you are buying clothes. As you cannot try them on, you may find when they arrive that they don't fit and you have to send them back. You also have to make sure that there is someone at home to receive the items you have ordered. Another important consideration when shopping online is security because when you are paying by debit or credit card it can be more difficult for stores to check someone's identity. Finally, shopping is a way of getting out and meeting others. For some people, shopping can be a means of socialising with friends and they could become quite isolated if they did all their shopping online.

So there are advantages and disadvantages to online shopping, but in my opinion it is the best way of buying things.

General Training Test 2

READING

SECTION 1

1 G
2 D
3 A
4 A
5 F
6 C
7 D
8 C
9 FALSE
10 NOT GIVEN
11 TRUE
12 FALSE
13 TRUE
14 TRUE

SECTION 2

15 gaps
16 motivation
17 questions
18 evidence
19 strength
20 feedback
21 clarification
22 competitors
23 regulations
24 finance
25 referrals
26 associations
27 records

SECTION 3

28 vii
29 iv
30 v
31 ii
32 ix
33 vi
34 courtship
35 harvest
36 bamboo(s)
37 B
38 B
39 C
40 D

WRITING MODEL ANSWERS

TASK 1

Dear Sir,

I am a student from Spain and I have just completed a ten-week intensive Business English course at your college.

First of all, I would like to say that I thought the teachers were excellent. They were always well-prepared for lessons and it was clear that their knowledge of all aspects of business was thorough and up-to-date. The course book was interesting and contained a great deal of useful new vocabulary which was relevant to my needs. However, I was not happy about the number of students in the class. The brochure stated a maximum of eight but there were ten students in my class, which meant there wasn't enough space in the classroom.

Also, I was not very impressed with the resources – the computers kept breaking down and the internet connection was not reliable.

I would recommend ensuring that you do not enrol too many students. I would also suggest that you invest in new computers and install a reliable internet connection. I hope you find my comments helpful.

Yours faithfully,

TASK 2

It is clear that the use of the car has increased greatly over the past thirty years. There are a number of reasons for this. Firstly, technology has developed and it has become much cheaper to produce cars. Consequently, they have become much more affordable. Secondly, a lot of money has been invested in the improvement of roads and this has made driving much quicker and easier. Another reason for increased car use is that people are travelling further to work than they used to.

However, these developments have resulted in a number of negative effects. To begin with, by using their cars people have generally become lazier and less fit as they are walking less. In addition, there has been a rise in certain health problems, such as asthma, caused by the exhaust fumes that are produced. The main problem, though, has been the damage to the environment caused by the pollution resulting from these exhaust fumes. There is no doubt that car use has contributed to global warming, though in recent years steps have been taken to reduce the impact.

These problems mean that governments are now having to think of ways of discouraging people from driving. One way is to introduce a congestion charge and another is to raise car parking charges. Probably the best solution, though, is to encourage the use of public transport. The measures that governments can take to do this include making sure that provision of public transport is adequate, both in the cities and in the countryside. They can also ensure that it runs efficiently and that fares are reasonable, so that using public transport is a cheaper and more convenient option than taking the car.

Audioscripts
Test 1

SECTION 1

Man Montrose School of Photography.

Woman Hi, I saw your advert in the paper this week about photography courses. I just wondered what level the course is – is it for professionals or …?

Man Well, we run courses for all levels, right up to advanced. As we're almost at the start of term, most of the courses are full, but we do have a few places on the course for beginners, which is the one you saw advertised.

Woman Oh, great. That's what I was looking for. It is a part-time course, isn't it? On Monday evenings?

Man That's right. It's from 8 to 10 p.m. We run the same course on Tuesday afternoons in the summer, but not at this time of year.

Woman OK. And it starts on September the 9th, is that right? Or is it the 16th?

Man Actually, the course itself starts on the 23rd, but before that we're holding a taster session on the 16th. That's when you can come along and see whether the course is something you might be interested in before you invest your money in the whole ten-week course.

Woman Oh, that's a good idea. And is there a charge for the taster session?

Man Yes, it's £25 for the three-hour introductory session. The full programme is £215 for ten, two-hour sessions, which comes to £21.50 per session.

Woman Sounds good. You're a bit cheaper than some of the other schools I've spoken to in the area. Are you still on London Avenue?

Man The main school is, yes, but the studios where your course will take place are on Crabtree Road.

Woman Oh, right. Can you spell that for me?

Man Yes, it's C-R-A-B-T-R-E-E Road.

....

Woman So, what topics does the course cover? I do have a camera, but to be honest I just point and shoot without really thinking about it. I'd like to learn how to use my camera properly, then my holiday photos will come out better!

Man Yes, that's what most people say. Well, the course starts with an introduction to digital photography as you might imagine. We don't cover the use of manual cameras on this course – most people don't want that any more, though if you are interested, we do run specialist courses for that.

Woman No, I'm not bothered about that. What I'm interested in is how to take good photos of, well, everything, really, not just people.

Man Well, the course covers that of course, but also buildings and nature. We work on developing you as a photographer – you'll learn about how your camera works, and also how to develop your own style. That's what will make your work more interesting.

Woman Oh, yes, I can see that. And what about trips – getting out and about with our cameras, taking photos of things. Is that something you organise?

Man Yes, we do two optional trips which generally take place at the weekend – these are part of the course, but you don't have to attend if you can't or don't want to, or whatever. One of them is aimed at photographing people going about their daily routines in the street – observing them shopping and so on in the centre of the city. That's just for an afternoon. The other trip is a full day – we take you to photograph birds and animals in the country park.

Woman That sounds fun. Actually, I've been along to your school before to see some of the student exhibitions.

Man We'll display your work, too, at the end of the course – that's if you decide to do it. We have a little exhibition where members of the public can come along and vote for their favourite photo. That's in our gallery. The winner can choose between getting a discount on another course or some designer photo frames to display their work.

Woman Great! Well, I'm definitely very interested. What do I need to do to register for the taster session? Do I need to come along to the school?

Man You can book a place now over the phone and just come along at seven o'clock.

Woman Great. Yes, I'd like to do that, please.

SECTION 2

Welcome everyone and thank you for attending this training day for your new job here at Torby Hotel. My name's Vanessa Marks and I'm the Human Resources Manager. You'll all be employed in different roles and I'm sure you'll enjoy them! The training day will consist of two sessions this morning and another two this afternoon, with coffee breaks in between. We'll start the morning session by showing you round and then we'll come back to this room.

Torby Hotel has been open for over twenty years and we pride ourselves on offering an excellent quality service. Many hotels say they want their customers to feel as comfortable at the hotel as they are in their own home. We think people want to feel like they're away from it all, and we provide our visitors with a personal service and a bit of luxury they wouldn't normally have, which is what keeps them coming back. And it's just as important to us that our employees are as happy as our guests, so I'm sure you'll find the team friendly and supportive.

Now, I'm afraid there'll be a bit of form filling to do today! You should all have received a new employee pack through the post containing your contracts of employment by now – if you haven't, let me know. That should be signed and posted back to us. There's a medical questionnaire I'm going to hand out in a moment – you can leave that with me – and don't forget to send in your bank details form if you want to get paid! That should also be in the pack.

Obviously, health and safety is a very important issue in the workplace and it's something we take very seriously here. We had planned to have a short talk as usual from our health and safety officer. He's actually off work at the moment though so he's left us a film to watch which we'll do after looking at the employees' guide. This explains all the details of your employment, such as holidays, working hours, and so on. It shouldn't take long to look at.

We'll take a break for lunch at about midday and then we'll move on to some team-building exercises. You all have different life experiences and I know that, for some of you, this is your first ever job, so it's important to know something about who you're working with. Teamwork is essential when it comes to things like dealing with complaints from customers, for example, and feeling confident about turning to your manager for support when you need it.

I'm sure you'll have lots of questions about your role, so we'll end the day with a question and answer session. I'll also tell you what to expect on your first day of work. You met your line manager when you came for your interview, and on your first day, he or she will introduce you to the rest of your team, provide you with your uniform, and so on. The following day you'll take up your duties.

....

We want our customers to enjoy every minute of their stay at Torby Hotel and that's why we take pride in providing the best possible service. You've all been offered your jobs because we think you've got what it takes to do that. Being honest, punctual and reliable are important in any job – in the hotel trade, what makes an employee stand out is their ability to anticipate what guests need before they ask for it. This is essential to great customer service. Also, if customers do ask for something, make sure you know exactly what they've asked for. We're an open-minded team and we know that making mistakes is an everyday part of working life, and as long as you learn from the experience so you don't repeat it, your manager will be happy. We're always ready to listen to any ideas you might have about improving our service as well.

So, that's what we expect from you. What can you expect from us? Well, there are lots of benefits to working here at Torby Hotel. We pay a higher salary than most hotels in the region and allow our employees longer holidays at full pay to show how much we appreciate the work you do. In addition to this, you can take advantage of our facilities such as the gym and swimming pool at a discounted price. Meals are provided free of charge during your shift in the staff canteen, but we hope you'll eat in our restaurant at some point too – no reduced prices there, I'm afraid. We used to provide free accommodation at the hotel for anyone working away from home but we recruit locally now, so instead make sure you can get to work and home again easily and safely with our free staff bus.

OK, so if you want to ...

SECTION 3

Justin	Hi Myra. Sorry I'm late.
Myra	Hi Justin, it's fine. I've been reading through my notes for this project. OK. So, we have to design something ... an object that could be sold in the shops.
Justin	Yeah, and set out the project plan for it – the marketing, and so on.
Myra	Yes, I was thinking ... what about designing a new type of musical instrument – you know, most people like music and I've played music all my life.
Justin	Yes, we both have, but we also know that a lot of music is done on computers now.
Myra	But many people don't like that, do they? They think it's 'cheating'. I mean, I do really.
Justin	I completely agree. But we'd have to come up with a totally 'different' type of instrument and I'm not sure we could do that.
Myra	I know what you mean. What about something for children to play – they like making sounds to music.
Justin	You mean using cheap things like bells and drums?
Myra	Not necessarily. We could try to invent a simple stringed instrument, for example.
Justin	But even if we did that, it wouldn't appeal to that many people. Our customer base would be tiny, I think.
Myra	Maybe you're right.
Justin	It's a pity but ... um, you know what you were saying about children?
Myra	Yes.
Justin	Well, I do think it would be good to get into that market. How about designing a children's toy?
Myra	Now that's a better idea. Though people do get tired of seeing so many different toys in the shops.
Justin	Yeah, there are so many these days. People go 'not another new toy'!
Myra	It's a good market though.
Justin	Mmm. Parents and grandparents buy toys for presents, for birthdays, whatever.
Myra	Yeah, it must be such a profitable area of business.
Justin	And they can be very simple and cheap to produce, but expensive to buy.
Myra	Yes, and we both have very young siblings. We're surrounded by toys in fact, so we should find the creative side of it quite easy.
Justin	Well, we'll see, won't we? Is that decided then?
Myra	Yes, I think so.

....

Justin	OK, so now we need to agree a project plan – we need to discuss the stages in the design of the toy.
Myra	Why don't we draw a table and then we can divide the tasks between us?
Justin	That's a good idea. OK, so where shall we start?
Myra	Well, first of all, we need to find out what sort of toys children really enjoy playing with.

Justin	I know, my little brother's having a birthday party next week, so I could take him to it and have a chat with some of the parents while I'm there.
Myra	Yes, you'll need to have a few informal questions in mind.
Justin	I can do that. I can draft a few questions and take them with me.
Myra	I could actually produce a more formal short questionnaire and give it to the staff at the nursery my sister goes to.
Justin	That's an excellent idea. That should really help us decide what to focus on.
Myra	Once we know what we're going to produce, we'll have to think about the actual design as we need to produce a model, don't we?
Justin	Yes, well, I'd be very happy to get together a lot of different materials from shops and places around the area. I mean a lot of toys are made using plastic, but we would have to use something else.
Myra	Right, and I can put together a 3D model if you like. I could do it in cardboard.
Justin	OK. As far as making the toy is concerned, we're going to be given some help there, aren't we?
Myra	Yes, I don't think we have to worry too much about that at the moment. But we do need to think about the advertising side of things.
Justin	I think the best thing would be to design a commercial.
Myra	For radio or TV?
Justin	TV, I think. It's hard to demonstrate a toy on the radio!
Myra	Yeah. OK, we'd need to come up with the different scenes that will take place during the commercial.
Justin	Yes, we could discuss those first and then I could write it all up as a script.
Myra	It'll have to be very detailed so you need to include absolutely everything.
Justin	OK. Well, you may have to help me out with that at some point.
Myra	That's fine. It's a big job.
Justin	What else can we do?
Myra	Well, what about a poster?
Justin	Uhuh, it's a fairly traditional form of advertising. I guess the important thing will be that people notice it and it gives them the idea straight away.
Myra	Yes, it has to catch people's eye in some way.
Justin	Well, the critical thing is that it's colourful. Colour is something that people associate with children and toys and that's how it'll get noticed.
Myra	I completely agree. A lot of posters are black and white these days and that just wouldn't be effective.
Justin	So, shall we fix a date to review our plan and get started?

SECTION 4

Welcome to this lecture on the psychology of personality. Today I'll introduce the main theories of personality, but first, let's discuss what is meant by the term. A brief definition is that personality is made up of the individual patterns of thoughts, feelings and behaviours that make a person unique. Our environment and the situations we encounter also play an important role in determining how different aspects of our personalities are expressed.

There are several fundamental characteristics of personality. Personality is a constant phenomenon – people tend to react in the same way when they come across similar situations. For example, no matter how great our desire not to feel angry when we're woken up in the early hours by a car alarm or our neighbour plays his music at full volume, our immediate emotional response will usually be the same.

Personality influences our actions, too, and causes us to behave in specific ways. If a kid keeps bouncing his ball against the wall outside, unless we make a determined effort to behave differently, we'll probably end up yelling at him in frustration every time, rather than asking him calmly not to do it. Personality is shaped by both psychological and biological factors, and is expressed not only in behaviours, but through emotions and thoughts, which have an impact on our relationships and social behaviour.

What do we mean by behaviour, then? Well, it's how each individual reacts to the social and physical aspects of their environment. We all know people who seem a bit 'buttoned up' – who don't appear to express strong feelings such as joy or anxiety, whereas another person's responses might be dramatically coloured with facial expression, gesture and voice inflection. When psychologists examine behaviour, they do so in different ways. Some theorists believe that the internal characteristics of a person dictate their behavioural pattern, whereas others hold that the behaviour of a person is a result of the external situation in which they find themselves.

Of course, the way we present ourselves to the world and the way we are in private can be significantly different. How the world perceives us is a direct reflection of how we present ourselves to the world. Qualities over which we have little influence include our age, race and gender, but they certainly contribute to our personality because of how the world perceives us based on these features. The way we are treated can in turn affect our behaviour. For example, a person who continuously faces discrimination – because of assumptions society makes about him or her – may guard against this by coming across as cold or unfriendly. However, should we get to know him or her, we may discover a completely different person inside.

....

Physical attributes, which develop over time, also contribute to personality, and include mannerisms such as speaking softly or loudly, the way we walk, eye contact, and so on. If we speak quietly, for example, it's likely we'll be dubbed 'shy', whereas those with louder voices might be labelled 'extrovert', though in reality the opposite may be true! If we walk slowly, we might be perceived as relaxed, and in some cultures, if we don't look people in the eyes, they might think we're rude.

How we want the world to perceive us influences how we present ourselves to others. Characteristics such as attitude, response and general mindset create the surface of our individual personality. Attitude includes characteristics like friendliness or being standoffish; response is whether we're arrogant or thoughtful; and mindset concerns whether we're generally upbeat or moody, all of which hang together to create who we are. Remember, however, that the aspects of our personality that we choose to display may depend on who we encounter. The personality you exhibit around me – a professor – for example, is probably very different to the personality you reveal to your closest friends.

Dig a little deeper, and the private aspect of our being appears – our cherished dreams that might seem childish to others, our goals, and the moral code we live by.

Our ideas, daily internal monologue and thoughts are also elements that make up the person that only we truly know. And only we can decide when to share these parts of our personality with others.

Let's move on, now, to the different theories of personality …

Test 2

SECTION 1

Officer Good morning, Wessex Police department.

Sabrina Hi. Er, I need to report a theft.

Officer You've had something stolen?

Sabrina Yes, I have. Have I got the right number?

Officer Yes, let me just get a form … for theft … right, this is it. Let me take a few personal details first. Can you tell me your first name?

Sabrina Yes, of course. It's Sabrina.

Officer And what's your surname, please?

Sabrina Macarthur.

Officer M-C-A …

Sabrina No, it's M-A-C-A-R-T-H-U-R.

Officer Oh right. And can I have a contact phone number?

Sabrina Yes, it's 07188 233764.

Officer OK, got that. Now what is it that's been stolen?

Sabrina Well, I think the thief thought it was my purse, but in fact it was my reading glasses. They were in a soft case on the top of my rucksack. I didn't realise they were missing until I got to college and started doing some course work.

Officer I see. That must be inconvenient! Can you tell me how much they were worth?

Sabrina Well, I had them specially made about nine months ago and I paid £215 for them.

Officer And are there any special features that would make them easy to identify?

Sabrina No, not really. They're quite expensive, but they look quite ordinary. My previous ones were a bit special; they were silver and had a blue flash, but these were just brown. Quite plain, really.

Officer OK, I'll make a note of that.

....

Officer Right, let me take some details of the theft. Can you tell me when it happened?

Sabrina Well, it was this morning.

Officer OK, so that's today's date which is the 13th, no – just a minute, that's yesterday – the 14th of February, and what time?

Sabrina It must have been around 8:30 a.m.

Officer And where did it happen?

Sabrina Well, I only discovered them missing when I got to college. But I do remember someone bumping into my rucksack when I was at the station. I was waiting for a train and the platform was very crowded. It was the rush hour you see and there were a lot of people standing behind me and I was aware of my rucksack being touched. So, it must have been then.

Officer OK. Did you see the person who was touching your rucksack?

Sabrina No, I'm afraid I didn't. The train was late and I was starting to worry about missing my first lecture.

Officer I see. So, were there any witnesses? Do you think anyone saw the thief?

Sabrina Yes, my brother was standing behind me and he noticed someone near my rucksack. He didn't realise at the time that anything had been taken so he didn't mention it to me. But when I realised something had been stolen, I told him about it and he remembered seeing this person.

Officer I see, and so were you able to get a description of the person?

Sabrina Well, apparently the guy was quite tall.

Officer OK, good. Anything else? Any idea of age or build? What about hair – was it long or short?

Sabrina Don't know about the length but I was told it was black. I think that's about all I know, I'm afraid.

Officer That's OK. There've been a number of reported thefts recently in that particular area so we're trying to get a picture of whether a number of thieves are involved – or if it's just one or two. So any details, no matter how small, will help us. Has this kind of thing happened to you there before?

Sabrina No, it hasn't, but a friend of mine had something stolen a couple of weeks ago.

Officer And what happened then?

Sabrina Well, someone bumped into him. He didn't realise why at the time but later he discovered that his wallet had been stolen.

Officer OK, and did he report it?

Sabrina Oh yes.

Officer Good. Right, so just one last question. Are you insured?

Sabrina Well, I wasn't going to bother with insurance but we were given a talk about the importance of it when we started college, so fortunately I arranged some quite recently.

Officer Well, that was lucky. What kind of policy do you have? Are you sure it'll cover your theft?

Sabrina Yes, it should do. It's called 'student property' and it covers theft at home, when I'm travelling and also at college.

Officer OK, that should be fine then. So, we'll get in touch if we have any news.

Sabrina Right, thanks. Goodbye.

SECTION 2

Good morning everyone. My name is Katie Goddard and I'm the principal of Fairlight College. First of all, I'd like to take this opportunity to welcome all of you at the start of your studies here at Fairlight. We're a medium-sized college with approximately 2,500 students, 60 per cent of which are full-time. We also have a teaching staff of highly trained professionals totalling 127. The college buildings are about 50 years old and they were not initially used as a college. You may be surprised to hear that this site was originally a holiday village for about 40 years, and when that closed down the buildings were adapted to create the state-of-the-art college that we have today. Of course we do hope you have fun here, but we also expect hard work from you all. Most organisations and indeed many colleges have mission statements which set out their key objective. These are sometimes quite lengthy and complicated but we believe in keeping things simple here. Ours is 'Aim High', and I'd like you all to keep that in mind throughout your studies.

Our main purpose, of course, is to provide you with an education, but we also take seriously the need to prepare you for life and, in particular, for whatever you plan to do when you've finished your studies. Over the past ten years the college has worked hard to establish links with local industry in order to provide you with opportunities for work experience, both during your studies and afterwards. I strongly recommend that you take advantage of these opportunities.

And finally, you may have already heard about the Freshers' Ball for first-year students, but I'd just like to remind you that this is an ideal opportunity to relax and get to know each other. The date is October the fifth. In the past, we've held the ball on the college campus, but this year we decided to hold it in town at the Sunset Club. It's near the centre of town and is about three miles from the college. So, make sure you put that in your diaries.

....

I'd now like to point out a few important college facilities. I hope you all managed to pick up a map of the college campus on your way in. I'm not going to go over everything on the map, but I'd like to point out a few things that you should be aware of. So, first of all, I imagine most of you will have noticed the car park and the registration and admin building when you arrived today and which are at the bottom of your map. It's easy to find the sports centre as it's located conveniently by the playing fields at the bottom right on the map. The layout of the campus is very straightforward and there's basically a path that leads up

through the centre with facilities on either side. I'm sure you're all keen to get hold of your course books and I guess one of the most important places is the library. This is situated on the left of the main path just after the café.

I'd now like to draw your attention to a new addition to the campus and one which we're all very excited about. This is the Innovation Centre and is where we're hoping that all your creative ideas will produce some great new inventions. To get there, if you follow the central path past the orchard and then the arts building on your left, you cross the river and it's the new building on the right. The building on the left is the medical centre and if any of you have any medical conditions that we should be aware of, please call in here and register with the nurse.

OK, so I'd just like to point out the other two faculty buildings. To the right of the orchard and on the other side of the main path is the Science Block and the river runs behind this building. And next to this and further along the river is the Humanities Building. So, I think we've covered all the faculty buildings. Now, finally, you will notice the four buildings in the square in front of registration and admin. The two on the left I mentioned previously and on the other side of the path, the one nearest registration and admin, is the college shop and the other is the canteen which is open from 7:30 in the morning until 8 p.m. in the evening.

Well, I hope that helps to orientate you. If you have any questions please don't hesitate to ask me or any of the other members of staff, and I'm sure in no time at all this will all become very familiar.

SECTION 3

Tutor Come in Metin, how are you?

Metin Fine, thanks. I wondered if I could just have a word with you about my engineering assignment.

Tutor Yes, I've got a class in half an hour, but I can give you about ten minutes. I do need the other twenty minutes to get myself sorted out before I teach, though.

Metin That's fine. I just wanted to discuss some ideas with you.

Tutor OK. So, what aspect of building are you doing your assignment on?

Metin Well, I decided in the end to choose bridge construction. I had several ideas at the start, but I didn't want to focus on anything too modern. I wanted to opt for something that's been around for a long time.

Tutor Yes, I guess people have always built bridges.

Metin Whereas skyscrapers, for example, are great, but they're relatively recent constructions.

Tutor OK, well, that's a good reason. What aspect of bridge construction are you going to cover?

Metin Well, there are some amazing bridges in different places and countries so I thought I would start with some pictures, just a page or so of 'bridges around the world' and then go on to write about them.

Tutor That would involve quite a range of designs. It might be better to narrow your theme down a bit ... might make it easier for you to structure your work.

Metin Yes, I'm not very good at making choices.

Tutor You know, like a lot of students, you're trying to cover too much.

Metin Right, I see.

Tutor Plus you need to think about what you're being assessed on. Did I give you the outline for this?

Metin Yes, but erm, I don't think I have it here.

Tutor Well, last year's students will tell you that you won't do well if you only present an overview of something, it's not enough – no matter how many words you write.

Metin I see. You mean we have to show that we can go into something in detail.

Tutor Exactly. Perhaps it would be a good idea to have a re-think when you get home. Do you have plenty of books and articles?

Metin Yes, I've got them at my flat. My flatmate said I didn't need to bring them.

Tutor Well, it would have been helpful if you'd brought them along. Anyway, review all the literature you have first and that will help you develop your ideas.

....

Tutor So, which bridges have you read about already?

Metin OK. Well, I've read an article on suspension bridges ... you know, like the Golden Gate Bridge in San Francisco.

Tutor Uhuh. What do you find particularly interesting about this type of bridge?

Metin Well, I think a lot of people believe that they're a very modern steel-based structure but, actually, there were some very old ones that were made using grass that was twisted to form a rope.

Tutor They were often used to walk between mountains, weren't they? Very scary!

Metin Yes, um, arch-shaped bridges also go back a long time, um, they're quite interesting too.

Tutor Well, they go back to Roman times, don't they?

Metin Yes, and what I hadn't realised is that these ancient arch bridges were made without using cement to hold the stone together, so the builders needed some form of scaffolding to build the top part of the arch.

Tutor But that's still true today, isn't it? Despite all the modern materials we have, workmen still can't bring the two sides of an arch bridge together without having a framework around the arch while it's being built.

Metin No, so this basic principle hasn't changed much, even though they may look different today.

Tutor What other bridges are there you could focus on?

Metin There are beam bridges; they're about the simplest in terms of construction.

Tutor Just a horizontal surface made of wood, stone, steel or concrete and two supports.

Metin Yes, parts of these bridges are often known as 'girders' and people sometimes refer to them as 'girder bridges'.

Tutor Right, they're often most commonly used for trains and cars, aren't they?

Metin Uhuh.

Tutor And what about complex designs?

Metin Well, um a bridge called the 'cable-stayed bridge' is just amazing to look at. It's a bit like a suspension bridge but it only has one end or tower, and obviously a lot of cables going from this to the surrounding area.

Tutor Now, this is a modern bridge, isn't it?

Metin It is, although interestingly, I noted that there are sketches of it that date back to the sixteenth century.

Tutor And yet the first cable-stayed bridges were built in the 1940s, I believe.

Metin That's right.

Tutor Well, you obviously have a lot of knowledge already.

Metin Yes, and I guess I could select an ancient bridge design and a modern one.

Tutor Now that would be a good idea.

Metin OK.

Tutor So I don't think you need to see me again. I think you can select your material yourself this week.

Metin I would quite like to write it out and let you see it before I submit my final draft.

Tutor OK, you can email it to me, and remember to plan your assignment before you write it.

Metin I will! Thanks.

SECTION 4

Presenter Hello everyone, and welcome to this talk on the natural world. I'd like to start off by introducing our guest speaker, John Thompson, who'll be speaking to us about the behaviour and characteristics of birds called 'starlings', which are really quite astonishing. Over to you, John.

Lecturer Yes, thank you. Right, so starlings are a very common type of bird. They're medium sized and their feathers, although multi-coloured, appear dark and metallic looking. They're found mainly in Europe, Africa and Asia, but they do exist in most parts of the world. What I want to focus on today is a particular aspect of starling behaviour called murmurations. Now starling murmurations take place when large numbers of the birds gather together and form something that resembles a huge black cloud that swoops and swirls and spins in the sky. I'm going to describe when this happens and suggest why and how the birds do it.

So, when does it happen? Well, it starts during Autumn. Groups of starlings begin to gather in favoured places and these develop into murmurations that can comprise a few hundred birds up to over a million. The groups increase in size, as more starlings arrive, and reach their maximum populations in mid-winter, when migrating birds from colder climates join the main groups.

Why do they do this? Well, no one is really sure and there are several theories, but a possible reason is for protection, based on the principle of 'safety in numbers'. However, another theory is that it is to pass on information. As the starlings gather, their daily routine is fairly constant. Early in the day, groups of starlings go out to find feeding places. They can travel up to 40 kilometres each day, but the interesting thing here is that they always return at the same time each day. The murmurations can best be seen at dusk when the numbers are the largest and it may be that information on what they have discovered throughout the day is passed around in the evening.

So, as I said, these murmurations are astonishing to look at. The acrobatics and the displays are remarkable, but how do they do it? Again, no one is really sure but in the last few years a lot more progress has been made. In 2008, a team of Italian researchers conducted ground-breaking studies on the starlings of Rome. These scientists used a series of interlinked cameras to measure how individual shapes of starling groups change over time. They discovered that the birds changed positions in the group and took turns to be in front, at the sides, in the middle and at the back and that there were three basic rules: move in the same direction as your neighbour, stay close to your neighbour, and, as starlings can reach speeds of over 70 kilometres per hour, the third rule is the most critical and that is to avoid a collision. And, interestingly, the distance between neighbouring birds is much less than the distance of each bird from the one in front and the one behind. This is probably because starlings can see better to the side than straight ahead and having a larger gap in front and behind is rather like safe motorway driving, where cars need to keep their distance from the drivers in front. But even though the birds try to follow their neighbours as closely as possible, a tiny deviation by one bird is magnified by the surrounding birds. It is this that creates the impression of a huge cloud.

....

So, to end this bit, just a few notes on starling populations. Since the 1970s, in the UK there has been a reduction of 70 per cent in starling populations. In fact, the numbers of starling in the UK are a fraction of what they used to be and they are now on the critical list. For example, at Brighton pier on the south coast of England, murmuration sizes are now around 50,000 whereas they used to be up to half a million. However, we believe that numbers in the eighteenth century were also quite low because there is little reference to starlings in literature from 200 years ago – well, compared to other birds that were around at that time. It's thought that numbers grew rapidly throughout the industrial revolution partly because the weather was milder. And starlings are able to settle in new places quite easily. In 1890, an American decided to introduce all the birds mentioned in Shakespeare's plays to America. He released 60 starlings in Central Park, New York, and the birds thrived. There are estimated to be over two million starlings in the USA now and they can be found as far as the west coast. Now to move on to …

Test 3

SECTION 1

Beth Hi, is that the cycling club?

James That's right. How can I help you?

Beth I'm Beth. I've just moved to the village and have been thinking about getting involved with a cycling group.

James Hi, Beth. I'm James and I'm the club secretary. We're always keen to welcome new members!

Have you got much cycling experience?

Beth Not really. Does that matter?

James Not at all. There are lots of cycling opportunities here. For example, some of our members take part in competitions throughout the year if you're interested in that. Otherwise, we meet each weekend and just go cycling. We take a different route each time, ranging from easy to challenging, so there's something for everyone.

Beth Sounds fun.

James It is!

Beth Is there a joining fee, and what's included if there is?

James There's an annual membership. It isn't much, but it covers things like our newsletter which we email to members every few weeks informing them of what's going on. We also have regular meetings here at the community centre. There's a small extra fee for that to cover refreshments as well as any guest speakers who come along to talk to us about diet, avoiding injury, that kind of thing.

Beth Great idea, helpful for me to know about that kind of thing as an inexperienced cyclist.

James Oh, and if you do join we're giving all new members a free repair kit. We used to give a free water bottle for people's bikes, but most bikes come with those now, so …

Beth Oh, that's useful. Now, do you meet at the community centre before you go on rides?

James No, we meet outside the post office in Dougley.

Beth Oh. I haven't heard of that. How do you spell it?

James It's the next village. It's D-O-U-G-L-E-Y. The reason we meet there is because there's a large car park which is handy for people from outside the area who drive in.

Beth Got it. And what would I need to bring if I went on any of the weekend rides?

James Do you have proper cycling gear? There's a great local cycling shop which has some great offers on for our members at the moment. Long-sleeved T-shirts are very popular in this cold weather and I bet you've never tried warmers for your knees before, have you? And do you have a pair of cycling gloves? You'd be amazed by how much the right clothing makes a difference to your comfort and abilities.

Beth   I'm sure.

James   Well, the shop will sort you out with what you need. Anything else you'd like to know?

Beth   Yes. I have two kids. I'm not sure whether or not they'd be interested in joining the club, but they don't have their own bikes yet. Is it possible to hire them here?

James   Absolutely. We do everything we can to encourage people of all ages to take up cycling. You can pay monthly, which works out cheaper, or each time you attend a weekly excursion. It depends how often you think you'll be joining us on rides really.

....

Beth   I assume the rides you do are local?

James   Most of them, yes. We do longer trips when the weather's better. We sometimes stay away camping to make the most of it. One of our favourite excursions most summers is riding along the river as far as Brownside – that's about 100 kilometres away – though this year we're going to the mountains, which will make a change. At some point in the future we'll try the Lake District. That's something we've wanted to do for a while.

Beth   And you hold other kinds of events, too, don't you? I heard you do an annual charity event, is that right?

James   Yes, we do. We raised money for a new classroom at the local school last year through our sponsored bike ride. We have some other fun events too, like a party each year to celebrate the club's birthday. Members are welcome to bring their friends and family along to that.

Beth   Brilliant. Well, I think that's about everything. Oh, do you have the telephone number for the cycling shop you mentioned?

James   Yes, just a second … here we are. It's 221337.

Beth   Great. Oh, one more thing. It was my neighbour who told me about the club and suggested I contact you, but do you have a website where you put information?

James   We do indeed. Go to www dot, get outside – that's all one word – dot com.

Beth   Great, thanks.

SECTION 2

Presenter   And now for the last part of today's programme, I'd like to welcome author Erica Winter, whose recent book entitled *Say it in a letter* has already sold 10,000 copies. Over to you, Erica.

Erica   Thanks Mark. In today's world, it's easy to think that letters are a thing of the past. We rarely write them, and when we do, it's usually to a bank or an organisation of some kind. We no longer tend to write letters to our friends. Yet this is something I think we will come to regret; it's what I call the lost art of letter writing.

For one thing, letters used to consist of more than writing. Looking through some of my mother's old letters to me recently, I came across several that also had drawings in them. This wasn't uncommon in the past. Photos took much longer to print than they do now and so people often drew something to show what they meant. In fact, my mother still does this, not only in her letters, but also sometimes on the envelopes.

Another important thing about letters is that they represent one side of a conversation. And, before the time of emails, these conversations could centre on people's deepest secrets. As a child, letters would come through our door each morning from relatives and friends. As we got older, they became more personal. This made the letters important; it made you want to keep them. The ones I treasure I still have – they're tied up with ribbon and safely stored in a shoebox in my attic.

I get them out from time to time and read them and it's amazing because they remind me of how I felt all those years ago, what I was doing, who I was meeting, what I was looking forward to. And this is another thing about letters – they re-create the past rather like a diary. Yet they are more than that because they invite a response; emails will never tell us about the past in anything like the same way unless we print them off and keep them – but who has time for that?

....

So if you want to give letter writing a try – and in the years ahead, you may be very glad that you did – here are a few important tips.

First, using a pen and paper is very different from using a keyboard and a screen. We can't easily change what we write with a pen and so letters show much more of the thought process of the writer. And to get those thought processes going, you really need to make sure that the room you write in is a quiet one. And this means removing all mobiles, computers, tablets and other distractions.

Second, it's much more inspiring to write on decent writing paper using a fountain pen than it is to use an old notepad and a ballpoint pen. So make sure you have the equipment you need. It shows that you've taken the trouble to present your letter in the best possible way. Also, your letter will stand the test of time – cheap paper quickly falls apart.

As I said earlier, a letter is really one side of a conversation and because of this you may be asking your recipient – that's the person receiving your letter – to give you some answers to problems that you have. So in other words use your letters as a tool. If you're worried about your job, for example, you can consult others about the things that are bothering you and so get the sort of advice that you need.

You need to practise to make this really work for you, though. You need to think carefully about the wording of each question that you ask so that you get the answers you need. Unlike emails that we tend to write quickly without paying too much attention to wording, letters need patience and thought.

And lastly, make sure you know how to begin a letter; where to put your address and the date, for example, and how to finish your letter – depending on your recipient. Should you say 'best wishes' or 'yours sincerely' or simply 'love from'? The ending you use must be suitable or you might offend people. This will be something some listeners may have forgotten or never had the chance to learn in the first place.

SECTION 3

Man I'm really enjoying our Chinese language course so far, aren't you?

Woman Yeah, I definitely made the right choice coming to this university. The teaching's so good, isn't it? I love the methods our tutors use. They really get the most out of us.

Man I never thought I'd learn so much so quickly. Goes to show what a difference it makes being taught by native speakers. If I'd known about that in advance, it would have confirmed my choice absolutely.

Woman It's an aspect of the course which is really useful. It's cool having lots of options to choose from too, as far as topics to study is concerned, though that wasn't something I really considered in much detail when I was deciding where to study.

Man I know what you mean. I have to say, I'm finding the culture course absolutely fascinating. I'm glad that's on the timetable. By the way, how are you finding living away from home in a big city?

Woman Well, it was a bit of a nightmare at first having grown up in a sleepy village in the middle of nowhere! I do miss the peace and quiet sometimes, but I wouldn't have it any other way. I had to try something new.

Man That's why I'm here, too. There's no way I could live in the country. I'd be bored out of my mind. Do you think you'll spend the third year studying abroad? We have the choice whether or not to go, don't we?

Woman Why else would I have registered here? It's an unmissable opportunity, wouldn't you say?

Man I'm with you there. It isn't as expensive to do as some of the study-abroad programmes at other universities.

Woman Thankfully! Anyway, have you seen the list of study groups for next semester yet? We're allowed to join two. I'm having trouble deciding which ones to join actually. I'd like to do them all, though I know we won't have time, what with our regular lectures and everything.

Man Well, there's the grammar study group … my grammar could definitely do with a bit of polishing though I have to confess I'm probably likely to give that a miss.

Woman I've come to the same conclusion. The writing skills group would definitely be useful, especially if we end up working in China at some point.

Man I'd rather get my speaking skills up to scratch. You can never do enough practice there, so that's something I'm going to sign up for.

Woman I'll go with that. What about literature analysis? Fancy that? Getting to grips with Chinese literature sounds like a real challenge …

Man … and one I'll attempt at some later date, I think.

Woman I was thinking about putting my name down for it, though to be honest I might be better off putting some work into understanding what people are saying to me! So, I think I'll go for that group.

Man I know what you mean. That's that decided then.

....

Man How have you been finding the free online resources we've been given access to? I've found one or two of them useful, but some of them aren't as exciting as I'd expected them to be.

Woman Right. I tried the chat room the other day for the first time – you know, where you can make contact with real Chinese speakers and practise your language skills. I was chatting to a really helpful user called Mai. The connection was pretty poor though and I gave up in the end. I don't know whether it's always like that.

Man I had a similar experience, waiting ages for replies to come through. And what about the translation software? I've never been a great fan of it, but that stuff is really high tech, isn't it? It's got all sorts of functions, though maybe at the expense of getting a precise interpretation of what you're trying to say.

Woman You don't have to wait as long as you do for some translation software to do its stuff, but I think what you said is a universal problem with that kind of thing. Better to use our heads! What do you think of the vocabulary builder?

Man You know what, there's tons of useful and functional stuff to practise on there. I spotted several errors though if you can believe that.

Woman I noticed that, too. Maybe we should raise that with our tutors – let them know it's lacking in quality. We need top rate stuff at our level. The dictionary's not bad, but I've seen ones that have some interesting extras like activity sections – shame it doesn't have any of those.

Man I know. They can be slow to use though. The language lab's pretty lazy, isn't it?

Woman I've only used it a couple of times but I'd agree, there seem to be plenty of delays when it's setting up, though you can do some interesting things on it, once you've got it running. Then there's the writing checker – the thing you type into and it tells you what typing errors you've made. I got a bit bored doing the same thing after a while though, it's a bit limited in what it can do. I think I'd rather have my tutor's feedback.

Man   It would be better if it was a bit more interactive. Though how that would work I'm not sure. Anyway, at least we've got access to the resources. They're better than nothing, even if they're not perfect. Right, shall we look at …

SECTION 4

'Why are we studying this?' That's a question that as a high school maths teacher I was asked a thousand times, and one that you – as trainee maths teachers – will certainly be asked in the future. What is it that makes maths seem so difficult and unapproachable for many students? Getting good at maths is less a matter of brain power than staying power – the difficulty lies in the amount of patience maths requires. And it needs persistence too – it's not a subject that comes automatically or intuitively to many students.

Another question I used to be asked was 'How am I going to use this is in my life?' And this is the crux of the matter. Unless students can really get to grips with the relevance of maths to their everyday lives, it makes teaching the subject a very tough task indeed, especially when they know that in this world of instant gratification, they can find answers to virtually any problem by doing a quick internet search.

So what can we, as teachers, do to make maths more accessible and interesting to our students? Well, for a start we need to help them see how maths is needed in their daily interactions. Whether it's following a recipe or deciding how much paint you need for your kitchen walls, we need to help students see that it's maths that's at work in achieving these goals. It's easy to see why simply forcing students to employ methods of memorisation or reciting formulas leads to a teacher's failure to inspire in the maths classroom.

Maths is a universal language. Anywhere you go you can interact with people in all walks of life and they'll understand you if you speak maths. The language of numbers can help anyone perform daily tasks and make essential decisions. For thousands of years, the same principles of maths have been practised by mankind around the globe. In order to get things done, especially in modern society, you simply have to employ maths. Your proficiency in the subject, or even a little knowledge of the fundamental operations of it can help you shop wisely and stay within a budget, or get your head round population growth.

Maths is also critical to a range of professions, and whatever your background, if you've been taught the basic operations of maths, you have the potential to become a millionaire. Just as literacy helps us get ahead in life, so does counting and the ability to make informed financial decisions. And it doesn't stop at work or daily transactions. Less obvious benefits of studying maths include other real-life applications such as the ability to learn to play a musical instrument, become a dancer or sail a boat.

....

So, what is it that we need to be teaching? Yes, it's difficult to see how some mathematical concepts translate to the world outside education. Perhaps you'll never use a particular formula in your job, but by learning the process, you'll have trained your brain to solve problems whilst reinforcing the basics of maths. There are, however, formulas which are more transparently useful – things like an ability to properly assess risk or statistics – things which even students should be able to see will equip them for the world beyond education. Maths makes our minds flexible enough to find solutions to complex, real-world problems.

Maths is a cumulative discipline – you have to gain an understanding in one area before you can effectively go on to acquire another. From the basic foundation of addition and multiplication to the complexities of quadratic equations, the only way to build a framework of knowledge is to learn step by step.

So, how did I answer that question – 'What is the point of doing this?' Until I got my students thinking about how they use maths to download music from the internet and hand over their cash for popcorn at the cinema, nothing I said made any difference. So, I asked them to imagine a life with no maths … that would mean no means of marking time with calendars or watches, no money or concepts like measurement. The idea of missing birthdays, not being able to top up their mobile phones, and a halt to the development of computer games made them open their eyes to the reality of life without maths. What better way to demonstrate the purpose of maths than to relate it to their own existence?

Moving on now to another aspect of maths teaching …

Test 4
SECTION 1

Jenny	Silverton Hall event booking, Jenny speaking. How can I help you?
Rob	Oh, hi. Um I'd like to book the hall for an event that I'm planning to hold.
Jenny	What date did you have in mind?
Rob	Well, I was hoping for the 15th of January.
Jenny	Let me just check. That's a Friday, isn't it?
Rob	No, it's a Saturday.
Jenny	Ah, just a minute. I'm looking at last year's calendar. Yes, you're right. We have something on in the afternoon I'm afraid, but the evening is free.
Rob	Great, I was hoping to have it in the evening.
Jenny	OK, and what times were you thinking of?
Rob	Well, the event is from 8 p.m. until 11 p.m., but I suppose we'll need to book it a bit earlier to set everything up and a bit later to clear up at the end.
Jenny	Yes, you will, so shall we say 7:30 to 11:30? Would that be OK?
Rob	Yes, that'll be fine.
Jenny	So, what kind of event is it?
Rob	Well, I'm organising a concert. Some of my friends and I play musical instruments so we're hoping to get together and we're inviting all of our friends to come along.
Jenny	Oh, that sounds like fun. What do you play?

Rob	The guitar, and my friend Jack plays several instruments.
Jenny	Great. So how many guests are you planning on?
Rob	Well, I'm not sure, but probably about 60.
Jenny	That's fine.
Rob	Thanks. Can I just mention that some of them are disabled? I assume that'll be all right and that access won't be a problem.
Jenny	Of course. We have special facilities and we've made some improvements recently as well.
Rob	Great.
Jenny	Um, so what about food? Do you have any thoughts on that?
Rob	Yes, I thought we'd have something simple. I don't want anything complicated like a buffet or a three-course meal. So, just sandwiches really and also something to drink if that's OK.
Jenny	I've got that. So, if you're playing music, do you have your own equipment? Because if not we can provide that for you.
Rob	Yes, we have our own equipment. We have our own instruments and microphones and amplifiers. We have everything except for a piano, which would be very useful. Would it be possible for you to provide one?
Jenny	Yes, of course. I'll make a note of that.

....

Jenny	Now, I don't know if you're aware but parking has become a bit of a problem around the hall. Well, actually, it's a problem all over the centre of town, and so we do offer some transport solutions.
Rob	Oh, well, we were planning on driving to the hall.
Jenny	Um, I wouldn't recommend that. But we do have a coach that will pick everyone up and take them home at the end of the evening. It costs a bit extra, but does work out cheaper than taking taxis. Would you be interested in that?
Rob	Yes, please. And I guess that would be easier than trying to park all our cars.
Jenny	It certainly would. Now I think I have all the details. Let me just add up the costs … That comes to £250, but I'll reduce it to £225 as we have a 10% discount from now until March.
Rob	Well, that's great, thank you so much.
Jenny	And now I just need a contact name. I guess that would be you, right?
Rob	Yes, that's right. It's Rob.
Jenny	OK, and your family name?
Rob	It's Jezowski. I'll spell that for you. It's J-E-Z-O-W-S-K-I.
Jenny	Thanks. And do you have a contact number?
Rob	Oh yes, hang on a minute. I haven't memorised it yet. Yes, here it is. It's 07232 855496.
Jenny	Great. I think that's everything for now. I look forward to seeing you on the 15th of January.
Rob	OK, thanks. Bye for now.

SECTION 2

Welcome to Coffee Incorporated, where you'll be starting work next week. Today's all about orientation, so first I'm going to talk you through the coffee processing that we do here at the factory.

Coffee beans are like a stone inside a fruit, and in what's known as the wet process, the outer covering of skin and fruit is removed before the beans are dried. Wet-processing involves the fruit being immersed in water in order to sort which fruit can and can't be used – any bad fruit will float and can be thrown out at this point. This reduces levels of pollution from dirty waste that some other methods produce – though admittedly some people do say the wet process reduces flavour, too.

After the fruit has been removed, we are left with the beans, which have to be dried to a water content of about ten per cent before they can be used to make coffee. We do this by machine – this is the way it's done where there are limits in terms of workspace, as is the case here.

An alternative drying method is natural drying, which requires the beans to be spread out on special ground areas or tables in the sun. The air is better able to circulate around the beans in the natural method of drying, but it does increase the number of workers required.

After the beans are dry, we go onto a process called polishing. This makes extra sure that the beans are completely clean. Some experts believe polishing damages the taste of the coffee, but that's a matter of opinion, and while polishing isn't actually required, we do it here to avoid the possibility of any remaining skin causing problems during roasting.

Once the beans are fully clean, they're sorted by size and weight. This is also carried out by machine. The beans are blown through the air and the ones that land in bins near the air source are the heaviest and best and will be made into the top-quality brands, whereas the ones that fall further away are likely to produce a poorer flavour – though they will still be used for blending and making instant coffee, and so on.

Beans can also be sorted by colour – this is the most difficult and time-consuming task as it's done by hand and needs workers with expertise and experience. Once the sorting is completed, the beans are roasted and stored ready for distribution.

....

In a moment I'm going to take you on a tour of the building and we'll see where all of those processes take place. First, I'll take you through to reception, where you'll sign in and out each day – this is important for fire regulations. That's located next to the visitor centre where we hold tours for the public. Do pop in one afternoon when it's open. As well as seeing the working part of the factory, we have a treat for you and that's the tasting room, where you'll get to try some of the products we make and which we sell a selection of in our staff shop. These are available to staff at a discount. For one day only you can choose something there for free as our welcome to you. Ordinarily we'd finish the tour with lunch in the staff canteen. It's being repainted at the moment so we'll have some sandwiches here in the training room instead.

I'm going to hand you out some protective clothing in a moment. Good to see you're all wearing sensible shoes which we requested for the tour, so thank you for that. There are some caps in the basket near the door over there. Please collect one, even if you have very short hair. They're essential in all food production areas these days. We won't be handling anything today, though ordinarily you'll be wearing gloves to work with the beans. In a moment I'm going to hand you out a badge with your name on – this is so we can get to know each other better. And hopefully you've all remembered pen and paper as I'll be giving you plenty of information to make a note of!

SECTION 3

Tutor Have you had any ideas about your dissertation proposal, Tim?

Tim I'm definitely doing something about saving dying languages – languages that are in danger of becoming extinct.

Tutor Sounds like an interesting idea. How are you going to focus your project?

Tim Well, my grandmother's first language is spoken by only a handful of people now, so I'd like to record an interview with her that can be kept in an archive – which she was really keen to do when I asked her about it. I know there are linguists already working on recording dying languages and when we focused on that in class I realised I wanted to do something for my grandmother's heritage. I wanted to discuss with you how to go about it.

Tutor You'd have to think carefully about what to include, of course, something about the impact of technology perhaps?

Tim You mean the fact that technology allows people to communicate at the click of a mouse across the world so it contributes to languages becoming endangered? I know this has resulted in lots of languages disappearing because people use international languages like English to communicate, instead of their own. That's why it's important to make an effort to conserve them.

Tutor So, in your introduction you could talk about the negative impact of globalisation on minority languages …

Tim Right, I'll mention that. And the media's had an enormous impact – schools teach in the standard languages of a country rather than minority ones. That means young people lose the language skills of earlier generations because they aren't exposed to them as they would have been in the past – I'll definitely put that in.

Tutor Good idea.

Tim I mean, take me for instance. I'm not a fluent speaker of my grandmother's first language so most of the time we speak in English.

Tutor Well, exactly. And then what are you going to say about how we can actually save dying languages?

Tim Well, I realise that there are organisations working to conserve them by creating libraries of audio and video material that document and conserve languages for future generations. That's what I'd like to contribute to – though I doubt whether it's possible to save my grandmother's language – there are so few people who speak it, I can't see why anyone would try to revive it – I don't think it's going to become anyone's first language again. Though if I do this, at least there will be a record of it.

Tutor And it may be that recording minority languages can save some of them from dying out.

Tim I don't get how, if no one's learning them as their first language.

Tutor Well, the data that's collected isn't just stored away and forgotten about until someone rediscovers it in the future. It can be used to develop teaching materials within communities so local children have learning tools they've never had access to before – you know, they can listen to and see these languages written down.

Tim Oh, right. I've also heard something about recording oral literature. What does that mean? Is it to do with how languages and culture are bound together?

Tutor Exactly. Team members from the organisations we're talking about travel to remote communities and record their stories, rituals, songs …

Tim … so it's not just language that's conserved. I see. It's like some of the traditions in my family that have come from my grandmother's community. It's important to me to keep those alive too – hopefully I'll have my own grandchildren to pass them down to and even if my grandmother's language itself doesn't survive, then at least some of the history and culture will.

....

Tutor So, talk me through your plan concerning interviewing and recording your grandmother.

Tim I want it to be useful … I'm not sure what I should be asking her to talk about that's going to get the best language samples.

Tutor Well, let's discuss a few options. You don't really need to look at what linguists have already done in terms of translating your grandmother's language into English. As you speak the language to a certain extent it would be better for you not to use English. You want to collect samples of her speaking in her first language rather than asking her to translate things.

Tim So, once I've got some recordings, should I concentrate on looking at grammatical forms?

Tutor Well, not necessarily. A better approach would be to focus on certain words, especially those for things which people don't use any more like in the home or on a farm. One way would be to get her to recount tales from her childhood. If you ask someone for a word, they might not remember it, but it might pop out in a sentence if they're focused on something that brings up the word naturally.

Tim Like, my grandmother might not remember a particular saying in her first language, but if I ask her to talk about her life it might come up naturally in context?

Tutor Exactly. Childhood's a good topic – everyone has lots of memories they can talk about. And you'll get much more authentic samples if you get her talking rather than asking her to write things down or translate them. You will of course have to produce a written version eventually yourself but that's quite different.

Tim OK.

Tutor Now, what about the practicalities of doing the recording?

Tim I thought I'd do a few shorter meetings rather than one long one. I read something about that giving me some time to think about what we've spoken about and then I'll have a chance to clarify stuff afterwards.

Tutor Good, yes. Let the audio run and listen to it the same day – if you leave too long between recording and listening there might be some things you don't remember properly. It's not necessary to make a written record of it straightaway, though.

Tim Right. Do you think it might help to say when and where we did the interviews?

Tutor Without doubt. But keep it small-scale so it's easier to manage. Covering as much as you can seems like a good idea – it could lead to confusion though.

Tim Yes, I get that.

SECTION 4

Hello. Today I'm going to be talking about the history of the measurement of time – something we all take for granted now. These days we're able to measure time extremely accurately and there's global agreement on what the time is anywhere in the world. But, of course, this has not always been the case. So, when and how did it all begin?

Well, we can tell that prehistoric people from 30,000 years ago were aware of the changes of the moon as time went by. But 25,000 years passed before humans began to actually track time. There is credible evidence for this from around 5,000 years ago and they did this by observing not just the movement of the sun, moon and stars, but by measuring where these were in relation to the earth and, in particular, where these were in relation to the horizon. This was known as horizon tracking. For example, they noted the position on the horizon of the sun at sunrise and sunset and how these positions changed throughout the year. From this they were able to predict when the longest and the shortest days of the year were. Initially, this measurement was quite inaccurate and relied on suitable natural markers being on the horizon such as hill-tops, trees, etc. But measurement became more accurate and detailed when certain communities built markers specifically to view how the positions of the sun and moon

related to them. One of the best remaining examples of these is Stonehenge in England, which consists of a number of very large stones arranged in a circle.

OK, so let's have a look at the first clocks. It wasn't until around 1,400 BC that the first primitive clocks were used to measure length of time. These were water clocks and time was measured by filling a bucket with water which had a small hole in the bottom of it. As the water dripped out, the water level went down, marking the passage of time.

Early civilisations also used the sun to measure time. Sundials were used to cast a shadow from the sun onto a horizontal surface marked with lines indicating the hours of the day. As the sun moved across the sky, the direction of the shadow moved across the dial and the time could be read.

Early time measurement in China and Japan also involved the burning of incense sticks. The longer the stick, the longer it burnt, and so standard lengths were used to measure lengths of time. Sometimes a stick with a different smell was burnt at a certain point in the day and workers would know when to move on to the next task because of the change in incense.

....

Let's now look at mechanical clocks. The first evidence of these is in the late thirteenth century in Northern Europe. They were made of iron, rather large and heavy and the wheels of the clock were driven by a weight which slowly descended. Initially, mechanical clocks didn't have a clock face and just struck a bell every hour. They were also only accurate to the nearest quarter of an hour, but it didn't matter if the time wasn't quite right because there was only one clock in each community.

However, when people travelled to other communities they discovered the time there was different. This first became a real problem with the introduction of the railways in the 1840s. Up until then, sundials had been the most accurate way of telling the time, but these were dependent on shadows made by the sun and this was too inaccurate for producing timetables. This meant that there was a need for a nationally agreed time system and in 1847, the time at Greenwich in London was taken to be the point on which the national time was based. There was inevitably a lot of resistance to this in the middle decades of the nineteenth century. People in other places like Bristol, for example, wanted their own time and didn't want to be dictated to by London.

An even bigger problem came a few years later with the need for a globally recognised time system. International shipping at that time used maps on which Greenwich was the main reference point. As zero longitude passed through Greenwich, it was decided at a conference in Washington that all longitude would be calculated east and west from there. So then it made sense to use Greenwich to also measure time for the whole world starting at the Observatory at midnight. People could therefore be confident that when it was 8 a.m. in California, it was 5 p.m. in Paris every day.

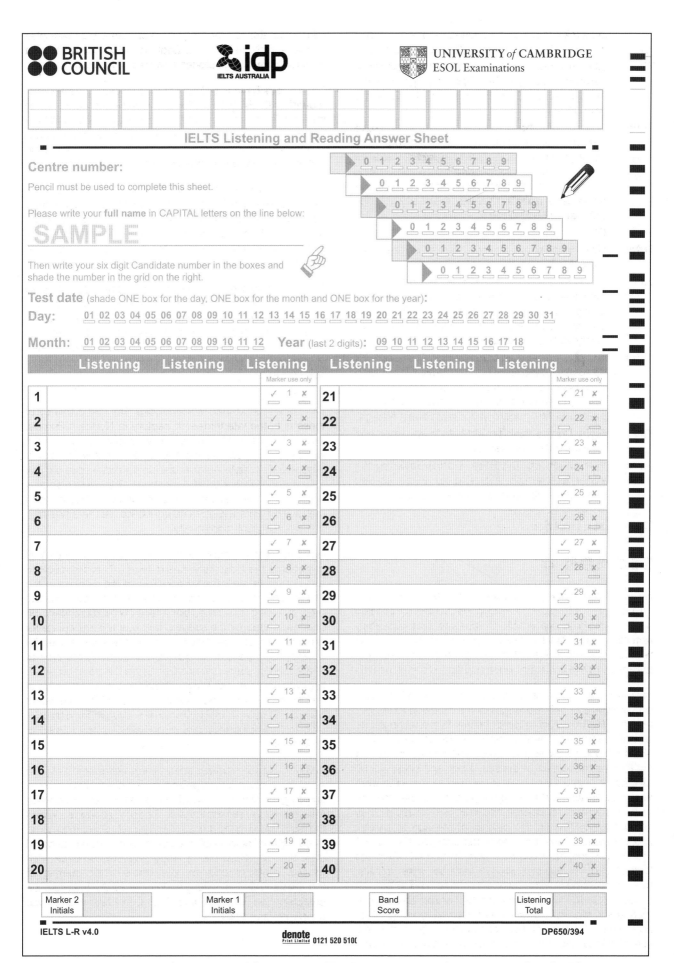

Exam answer sheets

Please write your **full name** in CAPITAL letters on the line below:

SAMPLE

Please write your Candidate number on the line below:

Please write your three digit language code in the boxes and shade the numbers in the grid on the right.

| 0 | 1 | 2 | 3 | 4 | 5 | 6 | 7 | 8 | 9 |

| 0 | 1 | 2 | 3 | 4 | 5 | 6 | 7 | 8 | 9 |

| 0 | 1 | 2 | 3 | 4 | 5 | 6 | 7 | 8 | 9 |

Are you: Female? ☐   Male? ☐

Reading   Reading   Reading   Reading   Reading   Reading

Module taken (shade one box):   Academic ☐   General Training ☐

		Marker use only			Marker use only
1		✓ 1 ✗	21		✓ 21 ✗
2		✓ 2 ✗	22		✓ 22 ✗
3		✓ 3 ✗	23		✓ 23 ✗
4		✓ 4 ✗	24		✓ 24 ✗
5		✓ 5 ✗	25		✓ 25 ✗
6		✓ 6 ✗	26		✓ 26 ✗
7		✓ 7 ✗	27		✓ 27 ✗
8		✓ 8 ✗	28		✓ 28 ✗
9		✓ 9 ✗	29		✓ 29 ✗
10		✓ 10 ✗	30		✓ 30 ✗
11		✓ 11 ✗	31		✓ 31 ✗
12		✓ 12 ✗	32		✓ 32 ✗
13		✓ 13 ✗	33		✓ 33 ✗
14		✓ 14 ✗	34		✓ 34 ✗
15		✓ 15 ✗	35		✓ 35 ✗
16		✓ 16 ✗	36		✓ 36 ✗
17		✓ 17 ✗	37		✓ 37 ✗
18		✓ 18 ✗	38		✓ 38 ✗
19		✓ 19 ✗	39		✓ 39 ✗
20		✓ 20 ✗	40		✓ 40 ✗

| Marker 2 Initials | | Marker 1 Initials | | Band Score | | Reading Total | |

Reproduced with permission of Cambridge English Language Assessment © UCLES, 2013